Walks
in
Nature's
Empire

The author at Spring Pond Bog

PHOTOGRAPH © JOSHUA SHELDON, 1994

Walks
in
Nature's
Empire

**EXPLORING THE
NATURE CONSERVANCY'S
PRESERVES IN NEW YORK STATE**

Scott Edward Anderson

THE COUNTRYMAN PRESS
WOODSTOCK, VERMONT

PUBLISHED IN ASSOCIATION WITH

ARLINGTON, VIRGINIA

An invitation to the reader

If you find that conditions have changed along these walks, please let the author and publisher know so that corrections may be made in future printings. Address all correspondence to:

Editor, Walks Series
The Countryman Press
PO Box 175
Woodstock, Vermont 05091-0175

Library of Congress Cataloging-in-Publication Data
Anderson, Scott Edward
     Walks in nature's empire : exploring the Nature Conservancy's preserves in New York State / Scott Edward Anderson.
     p.   cm.
  ISBN 0-88150-313-4 (alk. paper)
  1. Walking—New York (state)—Guidebooks. 2. Hiking—New York (State)—Guidebooks. 3. Natural areas—New York (State)—Guidebooks. I. Nature Conservancy (U.S.) II. Title.
GV199.42.N65A53 1995
796.5'1'09747—dc20   95-40
                                              CIP

Published by
The Countryman Press
PO Box 175, Woodstock, Vermont 05091-0175

Printed in the United States of America

Text design by Sally Sherman
Cover design by Karen Savary
Cover photo of Roseate tern, © Don Sias
Text formatting by Margaret Hanshaw
Maps by Alex Wallach, © 1995
  The Countryman Press, Inc.

For Anne,

Companion over mountains too numerous to mention,
guiding light through many a dark valley,
wonder-seeker in Nature's embrace.

Yet these sweet sounds of the early season
And these fair sights of its sunny days,
Are only sweet when we fondly listen
And only fair when we fondly gaze.

—William Cullen Bryant

THE NATURE CONSERVANCY'S PRESERVES
IN NEW YORK STATE

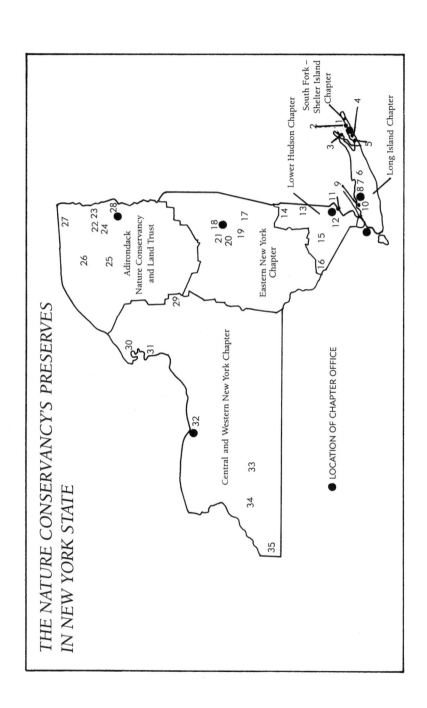

Lower Hudson Chapter

South Fork – Shelter Island Chapter

Long Island Chapter

Adirondack Nature Conservancy and Land Trust

Eastern New York Chapter

Central and Western New York Chapter

● LOCATION OF CHAPTER OFFICE

Contents

Preface
Walking New York

 I've traveled all over the Empire State, by virtually every means available: in buses full of hockey players, in automobiles on highways and back roads, and aboard passenger trains; I've flown over New York, swum its lakes, paddled its rivers, and hiked its mountains, hills, and valleys. It's a big state—the 30th in size in the Union, and I've covered many miles in my travels. No means of conveyance, however, has been so pleasurable as walking in New York—whether on city street, country lane, or woodland footpath.

This book is the result of walking through 35 of New York's spectacular natural areas. All but one of these areas are owned and managed by a group of professional and volunteer conservationists known as The Nature Conservancy.

Contained within these pages are descriptions and depictions of some of the finest natural wonders you can find in the state. No book can be so all-encompassing as to include all of the richness a state of New York's magnitude has to offer, however. As Wallace Nutting said in the introduction to his book *New York Beautiful*:

> A state touching the sea and two Great Lakes, Ontario and Erie, and having within it or bordering it Lake Cham-

plain and Lake George, with the Finger Lakes counted as five but in reality twice that number; a state with the vast Adirondack wilderness, as large as Connecticut, in the north, with the Catskill and Allegheny reservations beside; a state whose entrance is the Hudson and whose back door is Niagara; a state so overwhelming in the range of its attractions that it is little short of presumption to depict its beauties in one book—New York is worthy of a pictorial library . . .

For the purposes of this small volume I have focused on a select but representative group of some of New York's many charms. In these pages you'll find estuarine marshes on Long Island, a Hudson River tidal swamp, an Adirondack alpine community, numerous bogs and rivers, and a few exceptional ridge communities. Because it is virtually impossible to find a piece of land in the northeast that hasn't been influenced in some way by human activity, I have tried to impart a sense of the human history of these places, while at the same time offering an examination of the biological importance of these protected natural areas. A few of these—including the Adirondacks and most of Long Island—have been nominated for inclusion in the Conservancy's "Last Great Places" campaign, an ambitious conservation program designed to protect some of the earth's remaining intact ecosystems. Of course, these are all great places, after a fashion, which you will find out for yourself if you set out on any of the journeys described in these pages. After experiencing firsthand the conservation work fostered by The Nature Conservancy in New York, I am ever proud to be working for this organization as Director of Development of its Lower Hudson Chapter and to be furthering its endeavors. And make no bones about it, it is important work. Again, Mr. Nutting:

No state, whatever its natural charm, has arrived until it has recognized and practiced the broad truth that human activities must not mar the world; that they must supplement its charms and make it ten times more worth living in than it is now.

Acknowledgments

 I am indebted to all those who have walked and described these trails before me, including Katherine S. Anderson, Clifford O. Berg, Carol Brown, Mildred Comar, Natalie Goldstein, Carol Gracie, William T. Griffith, Peter Harriott, Laurie and Alan Holm, Ronald and Carol Killian, Bill Larrabee, Maggie Mann, Larry Paul, James Scheinkman, Mary and Michael Snowden, Debbie Tomlinson, and Peggy Turco. I am certain there are others to whom gratitude is owed, and I hope they will forgive my oversight.

I want to thank the many Conservancy employees who helped gather materials for or commented upon the text of this book, including Kristine Agard, Kelley Ahern, Carol Ash, Alane Ball, Tim Barnett, Sandy Bonanno, William Brown, J. Martin Carovano, Kathleen Conrad, Sara Davison, Stephanie Gebauer, Chris Harmon, Kate Hubbs, David Hunt, Peter Kahn, David Klein, Jane Lange, Mike Laspia, Fiona Lewis, Bruce Lund, Susan McAlpine, Debbie McGee, Melissa Mack, Olivia Millard, Peg Olsen, Kathleen Regan, Kathryn Schneider, David Tobias, Peter Whan, Robert Zaremba, and Andy Zepp. I am doubly indebted to Kathryn Kelly, who helped prepare the list of flora and fauna that appears as appendix 1 of this book.

Many of these preserves could not have been protected without the efforts of the scientists of the New York Natural Heritage Program, who identified many of these sites as significant.

Thanks also to Laura Jorstad, Susan Kahan, Carl Taylor, and Helen Whybrow of Countryman Press for their expert editorial guidance. Laura was especially patient and thoughtful during the process of seeing this manuscript into book form.

In addition, I owe a large debt of gratitude to the many friends who put up with the heat, bugs, overgrown brush, rains, and endless diversions while walking these preserves with me, including Valerie Boujoukos, Jack Langerak, Dr. Ellen Rosenberg, Thomas P.J. Rosenberg, and Joshua Sheldon. And to my wife, Anne, who put up with just as much as those listed above and more during the preparation of this book. Finally, I am eternally indebted to the late Gladys Taylor, who taught me that "the halls of learning have no walls."

🍂 *Scott Edward Anderson*
Lower Hudson Valley
September 1994

Foreword

 New York is widely known for its cultural diversity. It is equally endowed with a rich biological diversity. The Nature Conservancy has worked for over 40 years to conserve the best examples of the natural heritage that sets New York apart from all other places and defines the landscape in which we live.

The mission of The Nature Conservancy is to preserve rare species of plants and animals and the natural communities that support them. As a part of our strategy, we protect land—to enhance the survival opportunities of these rare species and natural communities. This preserve guide is an introduction to the successes of our work, a tour of important sites across the state. It is a way for individuals to learn more about natural areas in New York and to interact with plants and animals that are representative of our region.

Over the years The Nature Conservancy has changed with the times. We've grown from an all-volunteer organization to an international network with more than 90 professional staff members here in New York at 10 offices scattered throughout the state. Along with organizational growth has come an expanded conservation agenda, and these new perspectives allow us to make informed decisions on land acquisition and other actions to protect New York's biodiversity.

Our preserves represented in this guide are only some of those open to the public. Professional conservation stewards at our six chapter offices manage over 150 preserves. Each chapter now has a printed guide that describes our preserves and includes maps and helpful information about the biological features of the site and land management needs.

Our management of these natural areas is in some ways as important as the rare species we protect. We intend that our preserve system demonstrate good land management practices, those that foremost protect the biological integrity of the site but whenever possible allow human uses compatible with natural systems. The management of the dunes and beaches at our El Dorado Preserve south of Watertown provides one great example. The boardwalks at Silver Lake Preserve in the Adirondacks, Lewis A. Swyer Preserve south of Albany, and Sagg Swamp Preserve on the south fork of Long Island provide others.

In the last few years, as our staffing capacity and understanding of the biological needs of species and systems have increased, we have acknowledged that sometimes good conservation land management means we have to manage areas actively. Nowhere is this more evident than in the Albany Pine Bush where The Nature Conservancy has worked successfully with New York State and local towns to develop a cooperative fire management program to restore and maintain one of the rarest inland pine barrens in the northeast, home to the federally endangered Karner blue butterfly (*Lycaeides melissa samuelis*).

The High Peaks Wilderness internship program provides another example of the diversity of approaches The Nature Conservancy is developing to enhance biodiversity protection in the state. This is a cooperative program with the Adirondack Mountain Club and New York State Department of Environmental Conservation, designed to educate High Peaks hikers about the fragile ecology of our limited alpine meadows.

Even more recently, we have embarked on an ambitious effort to understand the management needs of larger landscapes, which include entire watersheds. Our new preserves at the Neversink River in Orange County and French Creek in the extreme southwestern part of the state are designed as education centers for the study of the processes that maintain the high quality of these streams. Both of these sites are part of the Conservancy's "Last Great Places" campaign in recognition of their global importance.

New York is an exciting place when surveyed for its range of beauty and biological diversity. Join us on the tour. We have only just begun. Much remains to be accomplished in our joint efforts to preserve the richness of New York's natural heritage.

❧   *Carol Ash*
    Regional Director,
    The Nature Conservancy of New York

Introduction

"Mother Nature's Real Estate Agent"

 The Nature Conservancy has been called "Mother Nature's Real Estate Agent," and with good reason. Operating in the United States for nearly half a century, the Conservancy has protected over 7.5 million acres of ecologically important lands and wetlands in this country. The Conservancy works only with willing sellers and donors, protecting land through gifts, exchanges, conservation easements, management agreements, purchases financed with the Conservancy's revolving Land Preservation Fund, debt-for-nature swaps, and management partnerships. Some acquisitions are transferred to state or federal agencies for management. Others are retained by the Conservancy, which manages each of its preserves using the most sophisticated ecological techniques available. The Conservancy owns and manages more than 1300 preserves—the largest private system of nature sanctuaries in the world. Its partner organizations have helped protect millions more in Latin America, the Caribbean, and the Pacific.

THE NATURE CONSERVANCY IN NEW YORK

From Montauk Point on Long Island to the Adirondacks, from

the shores of Lake Ontario to the densely populated areas north of New York City, The Nature Conservancy has been protecting land and rare species habitat in the Empire State since shortly after its conception in 1951. In fact, New York was the "birthplace" of the Conservancy's method of direct-action conservation. Its first project was organized by a group of concerned citizens in Westchester County who wanted to buy land in the Mianus River Gorge, and who contacted a group of scientists in Washington, D.C., that had come together as The Nature Conservancy for assistance. Under the Conservancy, they formed a subcommittee with authority to fundraise on the Conservancy's behalf. (Chapter 11 of this book describes the resulting preserve.)

The Conservancy now owns and manages over 150 preserves throughout New York, and is a thriving entity with more than 60,000 members across the state. This membership is served by the New York Regional Office in Albany, a New York City office, and six local chapters: South Fork/Shelter Island; Long Island; Lower Hudson; Eastern New York; the Adirondack Nature Conservancy; and the Central and Western New York Chapter. As membership thrives, so does visitation to the Conservancy's preserves. At Mashomack, on Long Island, the "Jewel of the Peconic" receives an average of 20,000 visitors per year. The Mianus River Gorge is visited by 10,000 people annually. *Walks in Nature's Empire* highlights the Conservancy's most significant and beautiful sites in New York. This guide offers both current and prospective Conservancy members, as well as the general public, a unique opportunity to learn about the wide variety of protection work fostered by the organization. For more information about how you can get involved with The Nature Conservancy in New York, see the membership form at the back of this book.

NEW YORK NATURAL HERITAGE PROGRAM

The New York Natural Heritage Program (NHP) was established in 1984 as a cooperative effort between the New York State De-

Baltimore butterflies (*Euphydryas phaeton*) at Thousand Acre Swamp

partment of Environmental Conservation (DEC) and The Nature Conservancy. Much of the initial support for this program came from taxpayers, through voluntary "Return a Gift to Wildlife" donations on state income tax returns. Current funding comes from the DEC's division of Fish and Wildlife and from the Conservancy.

The objective of the NHP is to establish and maintain an inventory of the location and status of New York's rare plant and animal species, as well as the highest quality examples of all our natural communities. This database is used to develop environmental impact statements, for land use planning, and in the government permit process. The information is crucial to helping planners, developers, state agencies, and The Nature Conservancy foresee the effects of alternative courses of action before making commitments to develop or preserve lands and wetlands.

The inventory relies on information from a wide variety of sources to keep its lists up to date. If you are traveling in New York and learn the location of a rare frog or moth, an endangered fish, rare grass or aster, or even a threatened wetland area, contact the Natural Heritage Program (see appendix 2) so that the information can be confirmed and entered into the database for future reference.

VISITING THE PRESERVES

Please observe the following guidelines when visiting The Nature Conservancy's preserves, or any other natural area:

1. Please practice low-impact visitation at all natural areas in New York; leave only your footprints behind and tread lightly.
2. The preserves are open from dawn to dusk throughout the year (unless otherwise noted) for hiking, nature study, birding, photography, and related activities.
3. Pets, bicycles, firearms, and motorized vehicles are not allowed on the preserves. Hunting, fishing, trapping, collecting of any species of plant or animal, fires, camping, and picnicking are also prohibited.
4. Some areas of a preserve may be closed during certain seasons, or for scientific or management reasons. Please note and obey any restrictions during your visit.
5. Please do not litter.
6. Groups of 10 or more should contact the appropriate chapter office before visiting a preserve.
7. While some preserves are handicapped-accessible (see chapters 17—Lewis A. Sawyer Preserve at Mill Creek Marsh; 24—High Peaks Whiteface Mountain Region; and 32—Thousand Acre Swamp), many others, due to terrain and other circumstances, are not.

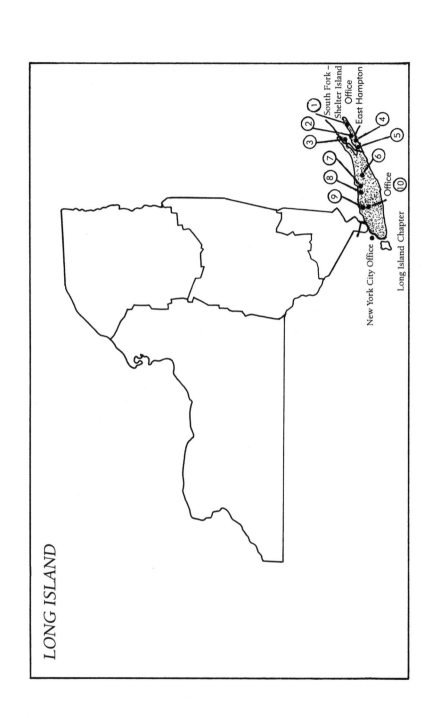

LONG ISLAND

① South Fork –
Shelter Island
Office
② East Hampton
③
④
⑤
⑥
⑦
⑧
⑨
⑩ Office

New York City Office

Long Island Chapter

Long Island

The Nature Conservancy has been working for nearly 40 years on eastern Long Island to protect the ecological resources that now fall within the island's Last Great Place—the Peconic Bioreserve. Working together, the two chapters on Long Island have already protected more than 25,000 acres privately and in partnership with governments, and own or manage a total of 41 preserves, including the Conservancy's flagship sanctuary, the Mashomack Preserve.

The Peconic Bioreserve encompasses the largest remaining undisturbed Long Island pine barrens and the watershed of the Peconic, the island's longest river. Unspoiled coastal plain ponds, acid bogs, and coastal plain Atlantic white cedar swamps characterize the Peconic River headwaters. The river flows east through the pine barrens to meet the Peconic Estuary at the town of Riverhead. Four interconnected bays link the estuary to the Atlantic Ocean and Block Island Sound. Highly productive natural communities occur here at and below the high tide mark. Salt marshes and submerged eelgrass beds provide food and shelter to commercially important finfish and shellfish of the marine waters. Sea turtles—such as the globally rare Kemps-Ridley (*Lepidochelys kempi*)—seals, whales, and countless shorebirds use the estuary for breeding or feeding grounds.

The Peconic Bioreserve habitats contain the greatest concentration of rare, endangered, and threatened species and communities in New York State. Of these species, 21 are globally rare; some find their last refuge on the earth within this area. At the ocean margin, pristine beaches provide habitat for piping plovers (*Charadrius melodus*) and roseate terns (*Sterna dougallii*), both federally threatened shorebirds. The Peconic Bioreserve also encompasses seven globally rare natural communities, including dwarf pine plain and maritime grassland. The pine barrens, the Peconic estuary itself, and the coastal ecosystem flanking the estuary form the basic matrix of the bioreserve. Collectively, these three contribute to some of the most scenic landscapes in the northeast. The interplay of sparkling ocean, calm bays, and dramatic coastlines has made this region one of the premier resort areas in the nation.

This guide also explores a few of the distinctive Long Island preserves that lie outside of the Peconic Bioreserve.

1 Montauk Mountain Preserve

MONTAUK, SUFFOLK COUNTY

9.24 ACRES (plus an additional 7.2 under registry and management agreement)

 Montauk Mountain Preserve is actually a hill with one of the finest examples of maritime grassland and heathland in New York. These terrestrial communities were once commonplace along the glaciated plains and moraines of the Atlantic coastal plain, but most have since fallen to the effects of residential encroachment and natural succession. Both maritime grasslands and heathlands are subject to the influence of offshore winds and salt spray, and their occurrence together provides for a unique combination of grasses and shrubs.

Among the more important species found at Montauk Mountain is the rare Nantucket shadbush (*Amelanchier* X *nantucketensis*). Other characteristic species present here are bearberry (*Arctostaphylos uva-ursi*), a low-lying, "trailing" shrub with plump red berries and paddle-shaped evergreen leaves; false heather (*Hudsonia tomentosa*); blueberry (*Vaccinium* sp.); little bluestem grass (*Schizachyrium scoparium*); and common or wavy hairgrass (*Deschampsia flexuosa*). The post oak (*Quercus stellata*) is another distinctive species at Montauk Mountain, with its crown of twisted branches.

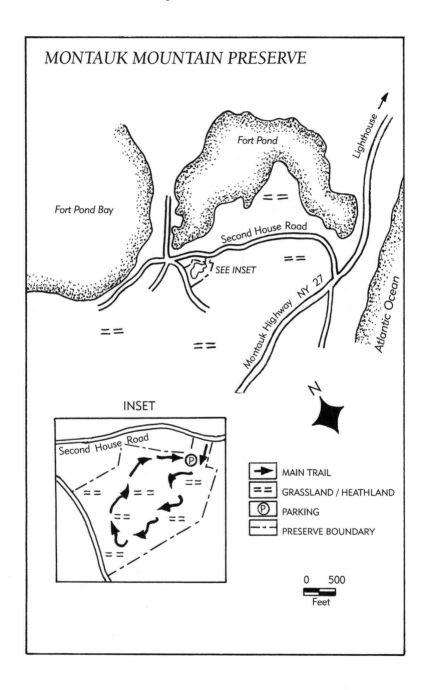

MONTAUK MOUNTAIN PRESERVE

Fort Pond

Fort Pond Bay

Second House Road

SEE INSET

Lighthouse

Atlantic Ocean

Montauk Highway NY 27

N

INSET

Second House Road

P

MAIN TRAIL

GRASSLAND / HEATHLAND

PARKING

PRESERVE BOUNDARY

0   500
Feet

Enter from the gate near the Conservancy sign and walk uphill to the summit. You are now 125 feet above sea level and here you'll gain a view of Fort Pond. Local legend has it that during the Revolutionary War, British ships anchored off Fort Pond were bent on raiding grazing cattle. Captain John Dayton, a "reckless, shrewd, and sanguine" individual, according to area historian The Honorable H.P. Hedges, foiled the attack by marching the local militia across the tops of the hills. At the completion of their file, the men turned their coats inside out and repeated the procession in the opposite direction. The British never attacked and Captain Dayton became a hero.

From the summit, bear right and down the edge of the hill. (Do not proceed straight, where the trail seems to logically lead, as this is private land.) The trail continues to wend downslope, passing some of the post oaks along the way, and eventually leads back to the parking area.

ACQUISITION

The initial purchase was made in 1982, and this was followed by additional purchases in 1986 and 1990.

DIRECTIONS

Just east of the village of Montauk and heading east on NY 27, take a left onto Second House Road (opposite Old Montauk Highway). Proceed 0.6 mile until just before Ruschmeyer's Inn on your left and opposite Fort Pond. Take the first paved road on the left about 0.1 mile before Second House Road bears right and becomes Industrial Road. The parking area is up the hill a bit and to your left. (South Fork/Shelter Island Chapter)

MERRILL LAKE SANCTUARY

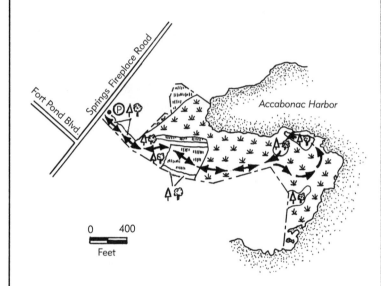

Springs Fireplace Road

Fort Pond Blvd.

Accabonac Harbor

0   400

Feet

N

⌂🌳	UPLAND WOODS
〜〜〜	PASTURE LAND
⚘	SALT MARSH
➤	MAIN TRAIL
Ⓟ	PARKING
---	SANCTUARY BOUNDARY

2 Merrill Lake Sanctuary

SPRINGS, SUFFOLK COUNTY
29.3 ACRES

 The Merrill Lake Sanctuary at the Conservancy's 200-acre Accabonac Harbor Preserve is a birder's paradise. The extensive, thousand-acre area surrounding Accabonac Harbor is an interconnected salt-marsh estuary that attracts both nesters and stopovers during annual migrations.

Merrill Lake offers many of the salt-marsh–related ecosystems found around Accabonac Harbor in a single concentrated area. This salt marsh was formed in several stages, beginning with the melting of the Wisconsin glaciation. As the sea level rose rapidly from the glacial meltwater, saltwater cord grass (*Spartina alterniflora*) established itself. Saltwater cord grass has an intricate root system that traps organic matter from the tides as they ebb and flow. The gradual accumulation of this organic matter caused the level of the marsh to rise, allowing salt-marsh hay or salt-meadow cord grass (*Spartina patens*) and spike grass (*Distichlis spicata*) to replace the saltwater cord grass. Although these two grasses are dominant, we also see glasswort (*Salicornia* sp.) and black grass (*Juncus gerardi*) at this level and, as the marsh becomes drier, species such as saltmarsh-elder (*Iva frutescens*), groundsel tree

(*Baccharis halimifolia*), beach plum (*Prunus maritima*), and bay-
berry (*Myrica pensylvanica*) take over. A transitional area, or ecotone, marks the farthest point reached by regular tidal waters,
where many additional salt-tolerant species like Canadian burnet
(*Sanguisorba canadensis*) and shadbush or serviceberry (*Amelanchier canadensis*) can be seen, as well as the beginning of an upland forest. This ecotone shares many of the same plants as the
higher hummocks or islands in the marsh, but still allows some of
the species of the marsh itself. Rare or endangered plant species of
the transitional areas found at Accabonac Harbor include silver-
weed (*Potentilla anserina* ssp. *pacifica*) and bushy rockrose (*He-
lianthemum dumosum*).

Look for signs of such mammals as white-tailed deer (*Odocoileus virginianus*), raccoon (*Procyon lotor*), and red fox (*Vulpes fulva*). Protected birds found at Merrill Lake include black-crowned
night herons (*Nycticorax nycticorax*), double-crested cormorants
(*Phalacrocorax auritus*), federally–threatened piping plovers
(*Charadrius melodus*), New York State–threatened common terns
(*Sterna hirundo hirundo*) and New York State–endangered least
terns (*S. albifrons*), and ospreys (*Pandion haliaetus carolinensis*).

Park in front of the gate and follow the footpath into a successional field. Here you will come to understand what Wallace Nutting meant when, quoting Shakespeare, he said the forest "knits up
the ravel'd sleeve of care," for it does indeed appear that this area is
repairing itself from the damage wrought by human hands. At the
edge of this field, and following the old colonial haying roads, you
will have your first clear view of the harbor. Proceed into a second
meadow and look for the osprey nests located high in poles near
the water's edge. You are now heading directly out into the salt
marsh and it can be wet, so take care. Look for the minute tubular
flowers of sea-lavender (*Limonium carolinianum*) among the salt-
meadow cord grasses.

Throughout the early 1900s, ditches were dug in Accabonac

PHOTOGRAPH © DON SIAS

Piping plover chick (*Charadrius melodus*)

Harbor as a means of mosquito control. This, unfortunately, resulted in a drying out of the marsh and a radical alteration and deteri-
oration of the natural productive capabilities of the marsh. Many
of the characteristic species of salt marshes were choked out and
supplanted by plants more commonly found in the higher and drier elevations. In addition, the spraying of DDT and other insecti-
cides—again to control our summertime nemesis, the mosquito
(*Aedes* sp.)—not only proved damaging to the ecosystem but,
when the mosquitoes built up defenses against the chemicals, this
method of mosquito warfare came to be seen as a costly error.

What, you might ask, are the natural productive capabilities
of a salt marsh? The natural benefits of a salt marsh, which acts as
a filter of nutrients and effluents, are enough reason to preserve
this natural community. Salt marshes have provided many benefits to humankind as well, beginning with the Native Americans.
The local tribes called this place "Accabonac," which to them
meant the "place where ground nuts are gathered." We surmise

that this moniker referred to a tuberous plant, *Apios americana*, that still grows around the harbor, and which the Native Americans used as a protein supplement to their usual diet of shellfish. Later, the European settlers harvested the salt-marsh hay for use as fodder, bedding, and insulation. They also benefitted from the abundance of shellfish and finfish in the harbor—and baymen can still be seen plying their trade there today. During the latter part of

SHOREBIRD PROTECTION

Once abundant on Long Island's shores, piping plovers (*Charadrius melodus*), least terns (*Sterna albifrons*), common terns (*Sterna hirundo hirundo*), and roseate terns (*Sterna dougallii*) nearly disappeared in the late 1800s as they were hunted for sport and for their feathers. Protected from hunting in 1918, the population slowly recovered, reaching a peak in the 1940s.

Today, the population levels of both species are lower than they have ever been. The development and recreational use of the species' essential habitat—Long Island's beaches—is the cause of the decline.

Federal, state, and public agencies, and private conservation organizations like The Nature Conservancy, are working to halt the species' population decline by locating, posting, and fencing active nesting areas while educating landowners and beachgoers. Full recovery, however, ultimately hinges on preserving natural habitats.

Some beaches where you can see nesting shorebirds:

- Cedar Beach, Town of Babylon
- Jones Beach State Park, Town of Hempstead
- Breezy Point, Gateway National Recreation Area

While you are enjoying Long Island's shoreline, please remember:

- Keep beaches free of predator-attracting trash
- Watch for and respect "restricted area" signs
- Do not linger near birds or nests
- Leave your pet at home, or keep it leashed

the American Revolution, the patriot militiamen used the harbor as a trading port for embargoed goods such as coffee and tea, and it was again a major link with New England during the Civil War.

With this in mind, now take a closer look at the salt marsh and the coastal areas of Merrill Lake Sanctuary. At the edge of the high-tide line, you will notice beds of eel grass (*Zostera marina*) and brown seaweed (*Fucus* sp.); these form a protective buffer for ribbed mussels (*Modiolus demissus plicatulus*) and periwinkles (*Littorina palliata*). The eel grass is also a major food source for Canada geese (*Branta canadensis*), frequent visitors to the harbor. If you examine the peat mat at the base of the grasses by the water's edge, you may see ribbed mussels, fastened by tiny byssus hairs, that form into something like a spider web. Once you have had a closer look and have rounded the harbor shoreline, you will be back in the heart of the marsh. Here you should take a right turn and retrace your steps to the gate. This walk can be accomplished in less than 1 hour, but allow more time for exploring this interesting natural community.

ACQUISITION

The initial parcels were donated by Mr. and Mrs. Frederic E. Lake in 1966 and 1968; the Lakes donated two additional parcels in 1972 and 1975.

DIRECTIONS

To Merrill Lake Sanctuary from Main Street, East Hampton (NY 27 East) bear left at the windmill onto North Main Street. Continue under the railroad trestle, past a shopping area, through the traffic light, and bear right at the fork onto Springs Fireplace Road (County Route 41). Proceed 5.5 miles, passing a white church, to the Conservancy sign on the right. Park on Springs Fireplace Road, enter through a fence, and follow the trail around the marsh. Waterproof footwear is recommended for all seasons at Accabonac Harbor. (South Fork/Shelter Island Chapter)

MASHOMACK PRESERVE

N

To North Ferry

Cartwright

Congdon's
Creek

Coecles Harbor

Foxen
Creek

FOU

Entrance

Visitor Center

Cedar Island

Sungic Point

Red

Route 114

Red

Yellow Trail

FOU

Fan Creek

Sungic Pond

Blue   Trail

Great Swamp

Gardiners Bay

To South Ferry

Smith
Cove

FOU Green Trail

Miss Annie's Creek

Log Cabin Creek

Green
Trail

Blue   Trail

Bass Creek

Nicolls
Point

Shelter
Island
Sound

Majors Point

Plum
Pond

Major's
Harbor

Northwest

Harbor

Mashomack
Creek

(P)	PARKING
⌒	DUNE
= =	FIELD
⬇	TIDAL MARSH
≡	BEACH
⬇	FRESHWATER WETLAND
⬇	BRACKISH WETLAND
🌳	UPLAND FOREST
■ ▪	PRESERVE BUILDINGS
⛺	GAZEBO
⚠	PLUM POND OVERLOOK
⚓	GARDINERS BAY OVERLOOK
🌀	RESTRICTED AREA - SENSITIVE HABITAT - NO HIKING ALLOWED

0   1
Mile

FOU   For Official Use Only

- - -   PRESERVE BOUNDARY

➤   MAIN TRAIL

3 Mashomack Preserve

SHELTER ISLAND, SUFFOLK COUNTY
2039 ACRES

The local Algonquin tribe, original human inhabitants of Shelter Island, had a name for this neck of the island surrounded on three sides by water; they called it Mashomack: "where we go by boat." Comprising a third of Shelter Island, the Mashomack Preserve is known to more recent inhabitants as the "Jewel of the Peconic," home to a large population of breeding osprey (*Pandion haliaetus carolinensis*).

Shelter Island itself is the largest in a series of glacially formed islands within the Peconic and Gardiners Bays. The Conservancy's "Last Great Places" campaign includes all of the Peconic Estuary, of which Mashomack is an integral part (see introduction to Long Island on page 21).

Mashomack has some of the richest natural habitats found in the northeastern states, including mature oak woodlands, interlacing tidal wetlands, freshwater marshes, and 10 miles of coastline.

The Pine Swamp complex at the preserve's western end, a series of hydrologically connected glacial kettleholes, is a noteworthy component of Mashomack's habitats. It has been designated a

Osprey (*Pandion haliaetus carolinensis*) nest
at Mashomack Preserve

freshwater wetland of "unique local importance" by the New York State Department of Environmental Conservation (DEC). Pine Swamp is named for the abundance of eastern white pines (*Pinus strobus*) growing there. It is thought that there may be a link between the number of ruby-throated hummingbirds and the lush Usnea lichens (*Usnea* spp.) that grow on the swamp's shrubs, including the locally rare mountain holly (*Nemopanthus mucronatus*). The Usnea, it seems, are a favorite nesting material for ruby-throated hummers.

Fourteen hundred acres of upland oak and beech forest on the preserve are now being allowed to mature into an "old growth" forest. These are interspersed with successional old fields and open meadows, which give the impression of the African savannah. Post oak (*Quercus stellata*) forms tangled thickets on the bluffs, exposed to the lashing winds and salt spray, while Mashomack Point's broad, windswept sand flats feature stands of red cedar (*Juniperus virginiana*), beach grass (*Ammophila breviligulata*), and prickly-pear cactus (*Opuntia humifusa*).

The unusual mix of tidal wetlands, surrounding bays, and tall oak trees makes Mashomack an ideal nesting place for the osprey. Until recently, ospreys were thought to be on the brink of extirpation, largely due to poisoning from the DDT used in mosquito suppression. Today they have already made a significant comeback. Ospreys gather dead branches, driftwood, and sticks from the surrounding area, which they form into nests piled high in treetops. They have been known to use the same nest each year and, consequently, human disturbance must be kept to a minimum.

A series of color-coded trails of varying lengths dissects Mashomack, including the Red Trail, a leisurely interpretive walk through Pine Swamp and Miss Annie's Creek, with views of Smith Cove. This is a 45-minute hike. For the more adventurous hiker, the 4-hour Blue Trail offers a stunning view of Gardiners Bay, from which you can sometimes see as far as Rhode Island, and from which you can gain a greater appreciation of the variety of Mashomack's natural beauty.

ACQUISITION

The Nature Conservancy purchased the Mashomack Preserve in 1980 from Aeon Realty Company. The Nicolls family lived on the land for 230 years (1695–1925); they sold it to financier Otto Kahn, who later sold it to the Gerards, who owned Aeon Realty.

DIRECTIONS

Take the Long Island Expressway (L.I.E.)/NY 495 to exit 70 South. Follow to the end and take NY 27 East (Sunrise Highway). NY 27 narrows from four lanes to a two-lane highway in Southampton. At Southampton, make a left onto County Route 52 (look for signs for North Sea and Noyac). Travel 0.9 mile to a traffic light and make a left onto NY 38. Travel 1.4 miles; make a right on Noyac Road (look for signs for Sag Harbor, North Sea, and Shelter Island). Proceed 7.2 miles to the Waterside Restaurant. Make a left turn and follow the signs to Shelter Island/North Haven/South Ferry. Take the ferry to Shelter Island; on NY 114 proceed 1 mile north to the preserve. The entrance is marked by a large wooden sign on the east side of NY 114. (South Fork/Shelter Island Chapter)

4 Sagg Swamp Preserve

SOUTHAMPTON, SUFFOLK COUNTY
89.01 ACRES

 If you start from The Nature Conservancy sign on the north side of Sagaponack Road, before you get to a small bridge, you will find a trail that offers a thoroughly enjoyable walk. You first enter an area of oak uplands that is very different from anything else you will see along the rest of the trail. Oak uplands are dominated by black oak (*Quercus velutina*), sweet pepperbush (*Clethra alnifolia*), and highbush blueberry (*Vaccinium corymbosum*). In the fall, Canada mayflower (*Maianthemum canadense*) exhibits a bright red fruit. Wood anemone (*Anemone quinquefolia*) and spinulose woodfern (*Dryopteris carthusiana*) combine with Canada mayflower to make up the predominant understory layer of this natural community. Look for a fallen red maple (*Acer rubrum*) near the start of this trail. Its complicated network of roots could not hold this tree upright during a storm—as you can see, there is little soil where it once stood.

As you proceed, notice how the flora of the red maple–hardwood swamp community begins to dominate. The transitional ecotone between these two communities, especially along the trail, features a number of interesting flower species, including gall-of-

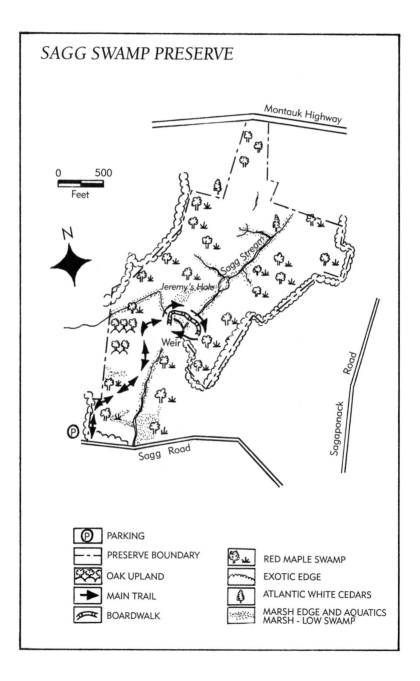

SAGG SWAMP PRESERVE

Montauk Highway

0   500
Feet

N

Sagg Stream

Jeremy's Hole

Weir

Sagaponack Road

Sagg Road

Ⓟ PARKING	🌳 RED MAPLE SWAMP
– – – PRESERVE BOUNDARY	∿ EXOTIC EDGE
OAK UPLAND	♦ ATLANTIC WHITE CEDARS
➤ MAIN TRAIL	∴ MARSH EDGE AND AQUATICS
⌒ BOARDWALK	MARSH - LOW SWAMP

the-earth (*Prenanthes trifoliolata*), along with blue lettuce (*Lactuca biennis*) and whorled loosestrife (*Lysimachia quadrifolia*).

The swamp has been in existence since before the first settlers arrived on the South Fork of Long Island in 1640. It is fed by Sagg Stream to the north and in turn feeds Sagaponack Pond at its southern end. In the late 1640s, annual "seapooses" or dig-outs to the ocean were formed from Sagaponack Pond, artificially maintaining the levels in this body of water and the adjoining marshlands. Wolves were said to be a problem in Sagaponack in 1651, but were soon extirpated through hunting. From this time until about the mid-19th century, various fulling- and gristmills were attempted at the head of Sagaponack Pond and the mouth of Sagg Stream. The last of these was launched by Jesse Hedges and John White in 1804, but by 1850, owing to a long history of economic failings, the mill closed and its pond reverted to swampland.

Sagg Swamp itself is dominated by an overstory of red maple; below this you can see spotted touch-me-not (*Impatiens capensis*), bugleweed (*Lycopus uniflorus*), and royal and cinnamon fern (*Osmunda regalis* and *O. cinnamomea*); the last of these are the most noticeable elements along this stretch of trail. There are at least 12 species of ferns found at Sagg Swamp.

Soon you will come to a fork in the trail where you should bear to the left. This spur leads to a beautifully crafted boardwalk that loops out over the swamp and eventually back to the fork. Be particularly cautious here, because the sphagnum muck is very treacherous. *Do not step off the trail or boardwalk.* This caution is meant as much for your own safety as for the protection of the bog. The local history is rife with tales of dogs and hunters getting lost in the swamp and slowly sinking into the muck, which can be as deep as 10 feet in places.

Within the swamp are three small groves of Atlantic white cedar (*Chamaecyparis thyoides*). Coastal Plain Atlantic white cedar swamps have largely been lost from Long Island, so this is an im-

Sagg Swamp Preserve

portant opportunity to preserve this rare natural community. The largest stand on Long Island is a grove of over 350 trees, many of which are over 100 years old.

Roughly 84 species of birds use the swamp in one way or another, and you might be fortunate enough to see the chunky, short-legged black-crowned night heron (*Nycticorax nycticorax*). If you visit in the early evening, listen for their distinctive call, a flat "quark!" or "guok!" The adults are the only heron that is black-backed and pale gray to white below. During our visit, we startled a siege of great blue herons (*Ardea herodias*) who were "bathing" in Jeremy's Hole, a pond at the preserve's center. Several varieties of hawks also use Sagg Swamp, including red-shouldered and red-tailed (*Buteo lineatus* and *B. jamaicensis*), as well as broad-winged and the smaller sharp-shinned hawk (*B. platypterus platypterus* and *Accipter striatus velox*). Osprey (*Pandion haliaetus carolinensis*) have been known to use the swamp as a breeding ground. Diverse groups of waterfowl are also in evidence. Among these are the blue-winged teal (*Anas discors*) and pied-billed grebe (*Podilymbus podiceps podiceps*), wood duck (*Aix sponsa*), mallard (*Anas platyrhynchos*), and black duck (*Anas rubripes*).

Once you have completed the loop and find yourself back at the fork, continue out to Sagaponack Road along the same trail on which you entered. This walk will take about 45 minutes at a comfortable clip.

ACQUISITION

The Nature Conservancy acquired 73 acres of the swamp in 1970. This and additional acreage was acquired through gifts from the following donors: E.J. Mathews, Caroll Wainwright and Walter Maynard; the Jemkamp Foundation; Sascha Gorodnitzki; John C. White; and Henry O. Golightly.

DIRECTIONS:

From Southampton heading east on NY 27, proceed past the traffic light in Bridgehampton and continue 1.1 miles; turn right at the next light onto Sagaponack Road. Continue south on this road 0.8 mile until you come to a small red schoolhouse on your right. Turn right just after the schoolhouse onto Sagg Road. Go 0.5 mile west on this road until you see The Nature Conservancy sign on your right. (South Fork/Shelter Island Chapter)

WOLF SWAMP PRESERVE

Scott Road

Millstone Brook Road

Elliston Town Park

P

Gate

C A

Steps

Big Fresh Pond

	UPLAND WOODS
	WET WOODS
	WETLAND SHRUBS
C A	CLEARED AREA
- - -	PRESERVE BOUNDARY
➤	MAIN TRAIL
→	SECONDARY TRAIL
P	PARKING

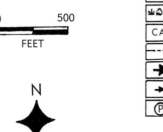

0   500

FEET

N

5 *Wolf Swamp Preserve*

NORTH SEA, SUFFOLK COUNTY
19.07 ACRES

 The Wolf Swamp Preserve, along with the 80-acre Elliston Park owned by the town of Southampton, protects a third of the border of Big Fresh Pond. Also known as Lake Missapogue, Big Fresh is a double kettle pond formed during the Wisconsin glaciation about 15,000 years ago. Until 1900, the only evidence of human presence on the pond was an ice house and a small camp and, until more recently, the north shore did not even have an access road. Development pressures have increased over the years, however, making protection of this area much more critical.

The gate to the preserve is locked, so you have to call the South Fork/Shelter Island Chapter office for the combination to the lock. (See appendix 2 for a list of chapter offices.) The main access trail goes to the right, which leads to a dry oak–beech forest that thrives on sandy soil. The porous nature of the ground allows nutrients to leach quickly, the result being a poorly anchored root system and a high susceptibility to fire. Black, scarlet, and white oak are the dominant species of this community (*Quercus velutina, Q. coccinea,* and *Q. alba*), along with American beech (*Fagus grandifolia*). Mountain laurel (*Kalmia latifolia*) can also be found here, together with blueberry (*Vaccinium* sp.) and dwarf huckleberry (*Gaylussacia baccata*), Indian-pipe (*Monotropa uniflora*), wintergreen (*Gaultheria procumbens*), and trailing arbutus (*Epigaea repens*). There are also several "indicator" species, like the numerous mosses and lichens that grow at Wolf Swamp, which point to the overall health of this ecosystem.

Notice the large uprooted beech tree along this trail. It fell as a result of hurricane winds. There are two other trees nearby that lean in the same direction, both fatalities from Hurricane Bob in 1990. The vegetation begins to change as you get closer to Big Fresh Pond, and you will likely see sweet pepperbush (*Clethra alnifolia*) and a member of the heath family, swamp azalea (*Rhododendron nudiflorum*). Here, too, you will find a path to a clearing and a set of steps leading down to the water's edge. Keep your eyes open for wood ducks (*Aix sponsa*) and migrating Canada geese (*Branta canadensis*). Eastern belted kingfishers (*Megaceryle alcyon*), black-crowned night herons (*Nycticorax nycticorax*), American bitterns (*Botaurus lentiginosus*), and canvasbacks (*Aythya valisineria*) have all been observed on Big Fresh Pond.

The pond itself is full of freshwater clams and fish. Banded killifish (*Fundulus diaphanus*), yellow perch (*Perca flavescens*), chain pickerel (*Esox niger*), and American eels (*Anguilla rostrata*) all migrate up Millstone Brook to Big Fresh Pond. Bullhead catfish or horned pout (*Ictalurus nebulosus*) also prefer the fresh water of the pond. Bullheads are the only freshwater catfish species found on Long Island.

If you retrace your steps to the trail from the pond and continue, you will enter the red maple–hardwood swamp community. This area will be noticeably different from the area around the pond. The red maple (*Acer rubrum*) and black gum or black tupelo (*Nyssa sylvatica*) trees of this environment have root systems that make them particularly adaptable to the extremely low oxygen levels of the saturated wetland soil. Some of the trees look like

Oak along trail at Wolf Swamp Preserve

they are built on stilts, which in fact they are: Their roots have formed a buttress spreading above the soil and never extend very far into the earth.

Pickerelweed (*Pontederia cordata*) and arrow arum (*Sagittaria latifolia*), both also called "tuckahoe," and bulrush (*Scirpus* sp.) can be seen along the swamp surface. Bluegill sunfish (*Lepomis macrochirus*) build nests at the roots of the arrow arum, which gets its common name from its large, arrow-shaped leaves.

Circumnavigating the swamp, you cannot help noticing the ever-present skunk cabbage (*Symplocarpus foetidus*) and Canada mayflower (*Maianthemum canadense*), as well as the ground pine (*Lycopodium obscurum*), which is a kind of club moss. Catbrier or greenbrier (*Smilax rotundifolia*), a thorny green-stemmed vine with leathery heart-shaped leaves and blue-black berries, climbs all over the trees in the more open areas. The trail will lead back to the gate (be sure to lock it behind you) and your tour of Wolf Swamp is complete. This tour can be accomplished in about 50 minutes, depending upon your pace.

ACQUISITION

Mrs. Elizabeth Morton Tilton donated the land in 1957.

DIRECTIONS

From NY 27 in Southampton, turn onto North Sea Road (County Road 52). Heading north turn left onto Millstone Brook Road and proceed past Elliston Town Park; cross West Neck Road/-North Magee Street to the intersection of Scott and Millstone Brook Roads. Park along the side of the road by the chain–link fence. Call the chapter in advance for the combination to the lock. (See appendix 2.) (South Fork/Shelter Island Chapter)

6 Daniel R. Davis Sanctuary

CORAM, SUFFOLK COUNTY
65.63 ACRES

 Part of the Ronkonkoma terminal moraine, the Davis Sanctuary is a fine example of a pitch pine–scrub oak barrens on Long Island. Between 8000 and 10,000 years ago, the last glaciers were in retreat, leaving behind pulverized rock and gravel. In addition, tidal storms and winds spread beach sand from the barrier beach over the entire Coram area. This type of soil is very dry, which is perfect for the pitch pine (*Pinus rigida*) and scrub oak (*Quercus ilicifolia*) that never grow higher than 15 feet at the preserve. If you look closely at scrub oak, you will see why it was once called holly-leaved oak (notice how the leaves resemble those of the holly). Other oak species, such as chestnut oak (*Q. montana*) and white oak (*Q. alba*), also thrive in this difficult environment.

Pitch pines have deeply penetrating roots that allow them to survive frequent fires. These curiously adaptive plants also produce new branches from their thickly insulated trunks when the outer layer is charred by fire. As a result, their form is noticeably disfigured, with twisted and gnarled branches that give them an eerie appearance. Pitch pines also reproduce using an elaborate system that includes both male and female cones. In spring, the

DANIEL R. DAVIS SANCTUARY

Residential

Logging

Logging

Private Lands

× 80

× 100

× 130

Training Lot

Militia 1812

Private Lands

Mt. Sinai Coram Road

N

0		800

Feet

– · –	PRESERVE BOUNDARY	△ COMMEMORATIVE TABLET
➤	MAIN TRAIL	✕ SPOT ELEVATION
·➤·	OTHER TRAIL	🌲🌳 PINE BARRENS / OAK FOREST
Ⓟ	PARKING	🌳 HARDWOOD FOREST
〰	WOODS ROADS	〰 FIREBREAK

tiny male cones produce a pollen that is completely dispersed before the cones shrivel and die. The wind-borne pollen fertilizes the eggs of the more recognizable female cones, thereby producing seeds. There are two types of female cones: open, which disperse seeds annually during their 2- to 3-year life cycle; and closed, or serotinous, which require extreme heat in order to open and release their seeds.

In addition to the soils being dry and friable, this type of natural community is dependent on fire, which has until recently been suppressed. The Conservancy now uses the latest controlled burning techniques to replicate the once natural cycle in a safe and manageable manner in a number of pine barrens, although not at Davis Sanctuary.

The other plants and animals in this community have, for the most part, also adapted to fire. Whether burrowing like the pine vole (*Pitymys pinetorum*) or developing waxy outer skins like the leaves of the bearberry (*Arctostaphylos uva-ursi*), there are many ways to avoid the pitfalls of fire-dependent living. The rare coastal barrens buckmoth (*Hemileuca maia maia*), for instance, buries its pupae deep in the sandy soil to ensure survival.

Begin walking west at the edge of the woods several yards west of the parking area. The field off to the right was once a training ground for the state militia during the War of 1812. You are now entering the pine barrens along an old woods road, which you will follow through most of the preserve. When you come to the second fork in the woods road, bear left (the trail is marked by yellow plastic blazes which have a green oak leaf and arrow printed on them). This will take you further into the barrens, where we saw quite a few hairy woodpeckers (*Picoides villosus*) in some of the dead-standing oaks.

The trail continues north-northeast before heading east and east-southeast after another fork—keep your eyes open for the trail signs. A footpath turns to the left off the road and takes you into the depths of the pine barrens community, eventually leading back to the militia field. Once at the field, you should follow along the edge of the woods back to the parking area. Please note that the field is not owned by the Conservancy, which has generously been given an easement to walk along its edge. This is approximately a 50-minute hike.

ACQUISITION

The first 40 acres were a gift of Charles J.R. Davis in 1964. Additional acreage was donated by Mrs. John G. Erhardt, Mr. Davis's sister, from 1968 to 1975, and by D. Davis Erhardt in 1988. The sanctuary was named for the land's original owner, Daniel Davis, great-grandfather of Charles Davis and his sister.

DIRECTIONS

From the Long Island Expressway (L.I.E.), take exit 64 and travel north on NY 112 for 3.4 miles. Turn right onto NY 25 (Middle Country Road) and proceed 0.2 mile. Turn left (north) onto Mt.

FIRE MANAGEMENT

Although lighting a fire in the woods may seem like the wrong thing to do, there is another side to this burning issue. Fires have regularly occurred for thousands of years in New York pine barrens and grasslands. These areas can not only take the heat (so to speak), they have actually evolved to require fire. Without periodic burning many species of plants and animals would be displaced by other species, and the unique assemblage that makes up these natural communities would be lost.

In recognition of fire's essential role in the survival of species and natural communities, The Nature Conservancy has established a national Fire Management and Research Program. Under this program, prescriptions for using fire as an ecological tool in the restoration and maintenance of healthy pine barrens and grasslands are being used on Long Island and throughout New York.

Sinai Coram Road and proceed 0.15 mile. Turn left into the drive-way at #16 (the sanctuary entrance is shared with this private driveway) and bear right toward the entrance gate. Open the gate, drive through, and park in the fenced parking area. Please be sure to close the gate before starting on your walk, and again when you leave. (Long Island Chapter)

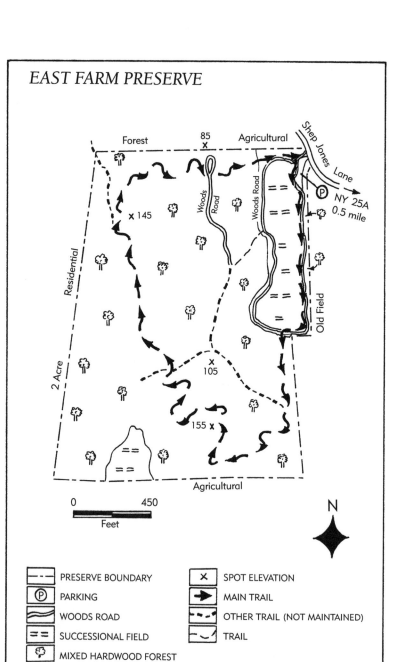

EAST FARM PRESERVE

Forest   85 ✗   Agricultural

Shep Jones Lane

Woods Road

Woods Road

✗ 145

Residential

2 Acre

Ⓟ NY 25A 0.5 mile

Old Field

✗ 105

155 ✗

Agricultural

0	450

Feet

N

PRESERVE BOUNDARY	✗	SPOT ELEVATION
Ⓟ PARKING	➤	MAIN TRAIL
WOODS ROAD		OTHER TRAIL (NOT MAINTAINED)
== SUCCESSIONAL FIELD	⌐⌐	TRAIL
MIXED HARDWOOD FOREST		

7 *East Farm Preserve*

VILLAGE OF HEAD OF THE HARBOR, SUFFOLK COUNTY
107 ACRES

 East Farm was working farmland for much of its 300-year history. Timothy Mills acquired the tract in 1693 and a long line of tenant farmers continued to work this land until as late as 1974. The preserve encompasses a quarter of the Mills Pond Historic District and was part of the Harbor Hill terminal moraine.

The Harbor Hill moraine is the most recent of the two significant glacial deposits on Long Island, the other being the Ronkonkoma moraine. As the glaciers moved south, the mile-thick ice lopped off the tops of mountains and hills in New England, grinding this "till" while pressing toward the sea. The glaciers halted as the climate warmed, and began to melt. The advance that resulted in the Harbor Hill moraine terminated not far into what is now the north shore of Long Island. It spans the length of the island, stretching from Greenpoint, Brooklyn, to Orient Point on the eastern tip of Long Island's North Fork.

Terminal moraines make for great variety when it comes to landscape and habitats, and there are at least three distinct environments at the East Farm Preserve. You will pass through each of these on the well-marked trails. Heading south on the trail from the parking area located on Shep Jones Lane, you will first come to a tangle of immature trees, Virginia creeper (*Parthenocissus quinquefolia*), poison ivy (*Toxicodendron radicans*), and the highly invasive Asiatic bittersweet (*Celastrus orbiculatus*), all of which indicate a successional old field.

After about 1000 feet you will enter successional southern hardwoods dominated by black cherry (*Prunus serotina*). Continuing up a small hill that rises 155 feet above sea level, notice the thick stands of large black birch (*Betula lenta*), hickory (*Carya* sp.), and tulip tree (*Liriodendron tulipifera*). Traveling down the western slope and heading north toward a second hill (145 feet), you will see oak (*Quercus* sp.), American beech (*Fagus grandifolia*), ground pine or tree clubmoss (*Lycopodium obscurum*), and mountain laurel (*Kalmia latifolia*). It is an interesting and characteristic mix of what is known as an eastern deciduous forest. This blending of old fields, hedgerows, and woodlands supports an assortment of small mammals common to northern Long Island, including eastern moles (*Scalopus aquaticus*), gray squirrels (*Sciurus carolinensis pensylvanicus*), and eastern chipmunks (*Tamias striatus fisheri*).

This is roughly a 50-minute hike.

ACQUISITION

Mr. Leighton Coleman donated this area in 1970.

DIRECTIONS

From the Long Island Expressway (L.I.E.) take exit 56 and travel north on NY 111 (Wheeler Road) for 1.8 miles. Turn left at the traffic light, continuing on NY 111 (now Hauppauge Road) for 2.3 miles to the junction of NY 25 and NY 25A. Proceed across NY 25 and onto NY 25A (North Country Road) and continue for approximately 4.3 miles. Turn left (north) onto Shep Jones Lane and proceed about 0.5 mile. The parking area is just off the road to the left in the preserve's northeast corner. Look for the Conservancy sign and the trailhead. (Long Island Chapter)

8 David Weld Sanctuary

 All of the land that makes up the David Weld Sanctuary originally belonged to the Nissequogue tribe of the Algonquins. The land
came into the possession of one of the area's early settlers through
an act of heroism. In 1659, Montauk Sachem Wyandanch's
daughter was kidnapped by the Narragansett of Rhode Island.
John Lyon Gardiner, who lived on what is now Gardiners Island,
rescued the captive daughter and the grateful Wyandanch gave
Gardiner all the land from Huntington to Setauket. Five years later the aging Gardiner sold the land to Richard "Bull" Smythe,
who settled with his sons at the mouth of the Nissequogue River,
where he founded Smithtown. The Smythe family farmed the
land until 1933, when they began to sell off some of the parcels.

Later, David and Mollie Weld discontinued farming and timber harvesting when they took over the property. Mr. Weld ex-
plored his interest in wildlife management, planting trees and rig-
ging up feeding stations to encourage animals and birds to return
to the land.

Located on the north side of the Harbor Hill terminal moraine
(see chapter 7), the David Weld Sanctuary includes 1800 feet of

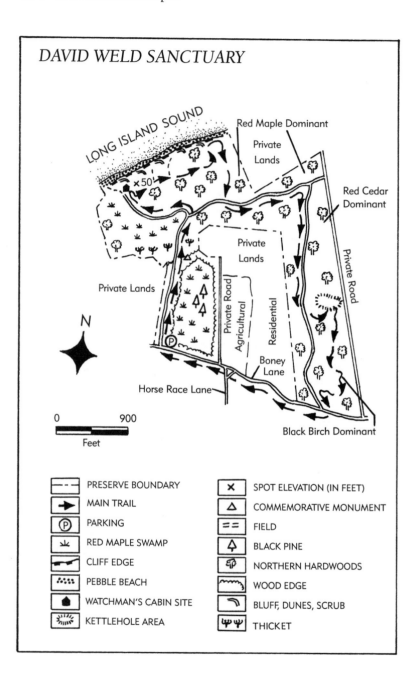

DAVID WELD SANCTUARY

LONG ISLAND SOUND

Red Maple Dominant

Private Lands

×50'

Red Cedar Dominant

Private Road

Private Lands

Private Road

N

Private Lands

Agricultural

Residential

Boney Lane

Horse Race Lane

Black Birch Dominant

0   900
Feet

Symbol	Description	Symbol	Description
- - -	PRESERVE BOUNDARY	✕	SPOT ELEVATION (IN FEET)
→	MAIN TRAIL	△	COMMEMORATIVE MONUMENT
Ⓟ	PARKING	= =	FIELD
⚘	RED MAPLE SWAMP	♤	BLACK PINE
⌇	CLIFF EDGE	♧	NORTHERN HARDWOODS
⁘	PEBBLE BEACH	⌒⌒	WOOD EDGE
⬢	WATCHMAN'S CABIN SITE	⤷	BLUFF, DUNES, SCRUB
⋇	KETTLEHOLE AREA	ѱ ѱ	THICKET

beach and bluff frontage. The sanctuary's once climax woods were extensively cut by a Smythe family descendant to make pasture during the early part of the century, but have now begun to return to transitional and climax woods. One of the trees you will see in the sanctuary is the tulip tree (*Liriodendron tulipifera*).

Also called tulip-poplar or "popple," the tulip tree is the tallest hardwood species in North America, and one of the most spectacular when it comes to displaying color. In spring its yellow-orange flowers resemble the blossoms of their family member, the magnolia. In autumn the tree's shiny green tulip-shaped leaves turn a brilliant gold.

From the parking area, follow the old road through an overgrown field and into the mixed hardwood forest. Bear left at the fork a little over 450 feet into the forest toward the edge of a high bluff overlooking Long Island Sound. From the top of the bluff (approximately 50 feet above sea level) you can see the Connecticut coast, as well as Eaton's Neck and its historic 1798 lighthouse. This lighthouse has the dubious distinction of marking the point where more shipwrecks have occurred throughout history than anywhere else on the north shore of Long Island.

At this bluff you will notice a flat spot of earth. This is where the "Watchman's Cabin" once stood. This cabin was built in the 1930s by the famous author and actress Cornelia Otis Skinner, who lived with her husband, Alden Blodgett, on land south of Boney Lane. Ms. Skinner constructed the cabin on the bluff so that she would have a peaceful place to write and rehearse her monologues. Legend has it that she would traipse up and down the beach and bluff while rehearsing "The Wives of Henry VIII." Only the legend remains of what must have been a fantastic place to work. Take the short trail to the bluff, then retrace your steps to the main path, turning left.

Dune-stabilizing plants such as seaside goldenrod (*Solidago sempervirens*) and beach or dune grass (*Ammophila breviligulata*)

Bluffs at David Weld Sanctuary

grow along the edge of the bluff, which you follow for a few hundred feet before heading back into the woods. At this point you will join another old road, which leads around the eastern "leg" of the preserve and through a tangle of red cedar (*Juniperus virginiana*), flowering dogwood (*Cornus florida*), and black locust (*Robinia pseudo-acacia*), which provide cover and feeding grounds for birds and small mammals. After a little over 3000 feet, a footpath off to the east will take you through the kettlehole area. The kettlehole was formed by a retreating glacier. Christmas fern (*Polystichum acrostichoides*) lines the slopes of the kettlehole and trailing arbutus (*Epigaea repens*) can be found on the floor of the depression.

The footpath then winds through the upland woods, climbing to about 100 feet before heading back to the old road. Once back at the old road, take a left toward the east parking area and proceed west onto Boney Lane back to your car. The entire trip takes a minimum of 1 hour.

ACQUISITION

David and Mollie Weld donated the original 42 acres in 1969 and another gift of 15 acres in 1971. Mrs. Weld donated additional parcels in the late 1970s, and two neighbors, the Woodys and the Millers, each donated additional acreage.

DIRECTIONS

From the Long Island Expressway (L.I.E.)/NYS 495 take exit 56 and travel north on NY 111 (Wheeler Road) for 1.8 miles. Turn left at the traffic light, continuing on NY 111 (now Happauge Road) for 2.3 miles to the junction of NY 25 and NY 25A. Go straight across NY 25 and bear left onto River Road. In 0.8 mile, proceed straight across Edgewood Avenue at the traffic light and continue for another 2.8 miles to the end. Turn left onto Moriches Road, which turns to the right after 0.1 mile onto Horse Race Lane. Go 0.4 mile and bear left onto Boney Lane. The sanctuary entrance is on the right at about 0.1 mile. (Long Island Chapter)

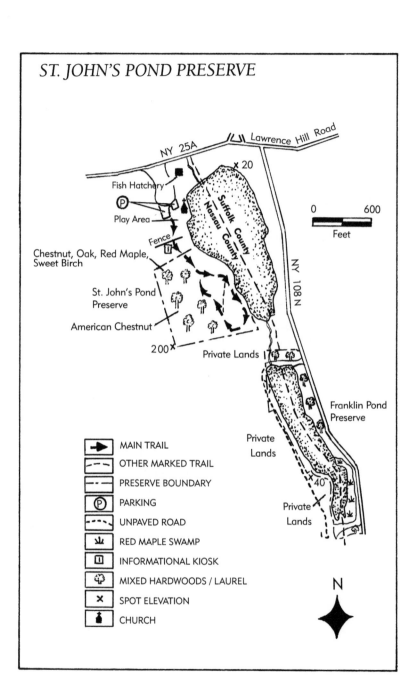

ST. JOHN'S POND PRESERVE

Lawrence Hill Road

NY 25A

×20

Fish Hatchery

P

Play Area

Suffolk County / Nassau County

Fence

NY 108 N

Chestnut, Oak, Red Maple,
Sweet Birch

St. John's Pond
Preserve

American Chestnut

200 ×

Private Lands

0   600

Feet

Franklin Pond
Preserve

Private
Lands

×40

Private
Lands

→ MAIN TRAIL

– – OTHER MARKED TRAIL

– · – PRESERVE BOUNDARY

P PARKING

· · · · UNPAVED ROAD

⚘ RED MAPLE SWAMP

▣ INFORMATIONAL KIOSK

⚘ MIXED HARDWOODS / LAUREL

× SPOT ELEVATION

⛪ CHURCH

N

9 St. John's Pond Preserve

COLD SPRING HARBOR, NASSAU COUNTY
14 ACRES

 St. John's Pond, along with nearby Franklin Pond, was part of a three-pond system (the third is now dry) that was created in the 1680s, when a dam was built to harness the energy needed to power grist- and sawmills. Merchants could ply their trade from Cold Spring Harbor, making this area an ideal spot for industry. Woolen mills opened in 1816, and produced fine textiles for post–War of 1812 America. After 1850, the industry here went into decline and, following the Civil War, the area became a popular summer resort. St. John's Episcopal Church was founded in 1835 to the north of the present preserve; the New York State Fish Hatchery and the Cold Spring Harbor Laboratory were both established around the turn of the century.

With its variety of habitat, including marsh, pond, and woodlands, St. John's Pond Preserve is a popular spot for nature study and bird-watching. Despite the longtime presence of human activity, there is a surprising abundance of wildlife at this preserve. Red fox (*Vulpes fulva*), opossum (*Didelphis marsupialis*), raccoon (*Procyon lotor*), and eastern mole (*Scalopus aquaticus*), along with several turtle and frog species, are all found here. Birds include broad-winged hawks (*Buteo platypterus platypterus*), great horned and screech owls (*Bubo virginianus* and *Otus asio*), along with thrushes, titmice, and even the ironically named common nighthawk (*Chordeiles minor*), a species listed as a "special concern" in New York State.

In early spring, look for the pink or white flowers of the trailing arbutus (*Epigaea repens*). For more local color in late May, mountain laurel (*Kalmia latifolia*) enlivens the mixed hardwood forest at the heart of the preserve.

You have to obtain a key to the preserve gate from the Fish Hatchery admission booth, which is open between 10 AM and 5 PM every day except Thanksgiving and Christmas. From the parking area next to St. John's Church, follow the trail to the gate. Be sure to lock up behind you and keep the key with you at all times.

The trail, which is actually an old railroad bed, leads into a mixed hardwood forest. In spring, keep your eyes open for blackburnian warblers (*Dendroica fusca*) and cerulean warblers (*D. cerulea*) high in the trees.

Bear left onto the trail that leads down a slope to the pond proper. Down by the pond you are likely to see a variety of herons, including great blue (*Ardea herodias*), green-backed (*Butorides striatus*), and black-crowned night herons (*Nycticorax nycticorax*), as well as both great and snowy egrets (*Casmerodius albus* and *Egretta thula*). Pied-billed grebes (*Podilymbus podiceps podiceps*) will dive to escape your sight at the pond.

The loop trail will bring you fairly close to the shore for 500 feet or so before it turns uphill into the woodland and eventually back to the parking area. This is a 30-minute hike.

For the best view of St. John's Pond, you can rest on the benches behind the church, or take a stroll on the church grounds. A visit to the Fish Hatchery is also in order when visiting St. John's Pond.

PHOTOGRAPH © THE NATURE CONSERVANCY

St. John's Pond

ACQUISITION

The sanctuary was acquired in two parcels, 8 acres purchased in 1968 and 6 more in 1973. Funds for the purchase of these lands were raised by neighbors wishing to preserve the sanctity of the area from encroaching development.

DIRECTIONS

From the Long Island Expressway (L.I.E.), take exit 48 for Round Swamp Road. If coming from the east, turn right at the traffic light at the bottom of the exit ramp to head north on Round Swamp Road. If coming from the west, turn left at the traffic light onto the road. Continue on Round Swamp Road for 2.8 miles and turn left at the traffic light onto NY 25 (Jericho Turnpike). Proceed 0.4 mile and turn right at the light onto Avery Road. Go 1 mile and take another right onto Woodbury Road; proceed another 0.4 mile and take a left onto NY 108N. Turn left on NY 25A and immediately left into the Cold Spring Harbor Fish Hatchery parking area. (Long Island Chapter)

UPLANDS FARM SANCTUARY

N

Entrance

Lawrence Hill Road

Private Road

Cold Spring Harbor
1 Mile

Field
Station

Barn
C.S.H.
Lab.

Start

Private

West Loop
Greenbelt Trail

Private

Office

Optional Return Trail

STATE
LANDS

Private
Lands

Residential

Massapequa
21 Miles

Residential

Saw Mill Road

Symbol	Legend
➤	MAIN TRAIL
==	OPEN FIELD
Ⓟ	PARKING
🌳	HARDWOODS (OAK, HICKORY)
⌂	CONIFERS
▨	RESIDENTIAL AREA (PLEASE DO NOT ENTER)
∿∿∿	HEDGEROW WOODEDGE (CHERRY, SUMAC, DOGWOOD)

0   400
Feet

10 Uplands Farm Sanctuary

COLD SPRING HARBOR, SUFFOLK COUNTY
93 ACRES

 This former dairy farm has served as headquarters for The Nature Conservancy's Long Island Chapter since 1971. The office houses visitor information about the Conservancy and a library, and sponsors field trips throughout the year. In addition to dairy cows, the fields at Uplands Farm supported sheep in the early 1900s, providing wool for nearby mills at St. John's Pond. (See chapter 9.)

The sanctuary features old open pastures along with upland stands consisting mainly of oak, maple, dogwood, and apple trees. Tangles of fox grape (*Vitis labrusca*), Asiatic bittersweet (*Celastrus orbiculatus*), and honeysuckle (*Lonicera* sp.) form a labyrinth along the ground and up into the low trees. The fields, which are mowed annually now that the land is no longer grazed, are filled with timothy (*Phleum pratense*) and orchard grasses (*Dactylis glomerata*), as well as many wildflowers, and are bordered by hedgerows of oak, hickory, and other deciduous trees. These areas are frequented by bobwhites (*Colinus virginianus*), ring-necked pheasants (*Phasianus colchicus*), and eastern cottontail rabbits (*Sylvilagus floridanus*).

PHOTOGRAPH © THE NATURE CONSERVANCY

Nature Study Program at Uplands Farm

Around the barn, you may notice the abundance of house sparrows (*Passer domesticus*), all of whom are descendants of those released into New York City's Central Park in 1850. American kestrels (*Falco sparverius*), sometimes known as sparrow hawks, also appear at Uplands Farm. These jay-sized falcons, recognizable by their rusty tail and back, hover over the open fields seeking their prey and calling out, "Killy-killy-killy!" Unlike other hawks, kestrels capture their quarry on the ground, and it does not necessarily have to be open ground. We have seen at least one kestrel pluck an unsuspecting sparrow from its perch within the rings of a chain-link fence.

From the trailhead, cross an open field and make your way to the second-growth forest. The area where the woods and field meet is called an ecotone. This is a term used to describe the transition between two different habitats. Here the diversity of plants and animals is high and an incessant battle for dominance is waged between the two natural communities. Left unchecked, woods will eventually choke out the field grasses and plants, because they offer a more stable environment. Invasive plants thrive in ecotones and here you can see the staghorn sumac (*Rhus typhina*), with its antler-like twigs and red terminal fruit clusters, eastern red cedar (*Juniperus virginiana*), and the ubiquitous Asiatic bittersweet (*Celastrus orbiculatus*), all of which will allow more shade-tolerant species to colonize the area. Ironically, the red cedar will eventually die out once climax species such as hickory, oak, and beech are established, as they cannot tolerate the dense shade created by these tall, leafy trees.

Follow the trail to the left about 800 feet and take a right turn that will lead you into the woods. Look for the ever-present arrowwood (*Viburnum recognitum*), which creates a dense network of archways dotted with creamy white flowers and slate-blue berries. This trail loops around for about 2400 feet. You then emerge from the forest and follow the hedgerows to the perimeter of the sanctuary. Continuing on this trail along the edge of another successional old field, you will eventually come to the West Loop or Green Belt Trail. This traverses private and state lands before circling back into a hardwood forest in the northwestern corner of the sanctuary and back to the entrance along Lawrence Hill Road. By the time you reach the Green Belt Trail, you have been hiking for about 20 minutes. If you are looking for a shorter hike, you can finish your loop before getting to the Green Belt by turning right at the edge of the first field.

The West Loop/Green Belt Trail, however, lets you see the remnants of the Harbor Hill terminal moraine. This moraine is the end-product of glacial deposits from over 15,000 years ago. Remnants of this glacial dumping are called erratics and have their origin in the rock formations of New England.

If you do travel this loop, pay close attention to the trail markers; there is a somewhat tricky switchback that needs to be negotiated in order to stay on course. (This misleading section is located off the Conservancy preserve in the southwesternmost part of the trail system.) If you are in doubt, turn around and retrace your steps to gather your bearings. The end of the trail winds through a hardwood forest, crosses a private driveway, and passes through a stand of pines before opening out onto the fields of Uplands Farm.

The entire hike, including the West Loop/Green Belt Trail, takes a little more than 1 hour.

ACQUISITION

The first 36 acres were acquired through a donation by Mrs. George Nichols, et al., in 1969. An additional parcel was purchased from Richard McAdoo and Walter Kernan in 1971, and the remainder was donated by Mrs. Nichols from 1972 to 1982.

DIRECTIONS

From the Long Island Expressway (L.I.E.), take exit 48 for Round Swamp Road. If coming from the east, turn right at the traffic light at the bottom of the exit ramp to head north on Round Swamp Road. If coming from the west, turn left at the traffic light onto the road. Continue on Round Swamp Road for 2.8 miles and turn left at the traffic light onto NY 25 (Jericho Turnpike). Proceed 0.4 mile and turn right at the light onto Avery Road. Go 1 mile and take another right onto Woodbury Road; proceed another 0.4 mile and take a left onto NY 108N. After 1.5 miles, at Lawrence Hill Road, bear right up the hill. Uplands Farm is the third driveway on the right, at the top of the hill. The parking area is to the left of the farm buildings. (Long Island Chapter)

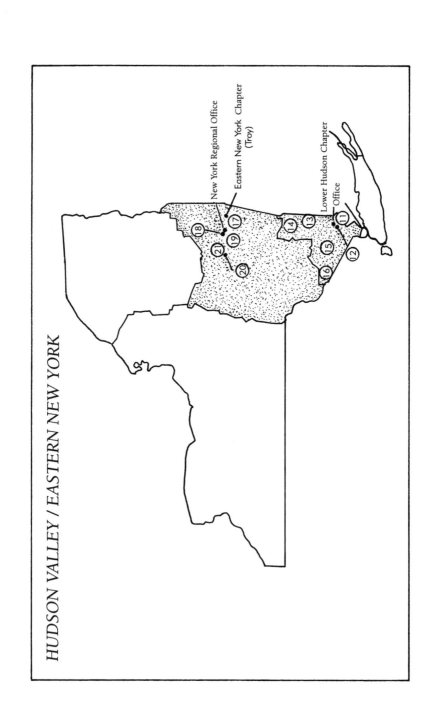

HUDSON VALLEY / EASTERN NEW YORK

New York Regional Office

Eastern New York Chapter
(Troy)

Lower Hudson Chapter
Office

Hudson Valley/
Eastern New York

The Hudson River valley and eastern New York region stretches from the northern shores of Long Island Sound to the southern shores of Lake Champlain. It encompasses the Taconic, Shawangunk, and Catskill mountain ranges, as well as the Hudson Highlands. This geological diversity is key to the biological richness of the area, but what ties it all together is the Hudson River.

The river is an important dispersal corridor for fish and waterfowl, and its tidal properties create a brackish and freshwater estuary that contains a number of globally rare species and natural communities, including tidal swamps, marshes, and mudflats. The Hudson River valley is also an important flyway for many species of migratory birds and raptors; it is also habitat for an abundance of mammals and reptiles. In addition, the valley has long provided livelihood and living space for Native Americans as well as the European settlers who came to the area in the early 17th century.

A correlative to this long history of human habitation is an equally long history of development. Cities and towns grew up around the manufacturing concerns that found the river an excellent resource for commerce and trade and the surrounding valley an ideal area for the business of living. "Quality of life" has been a bailiwick of communities throughout the eastern New York–Hudson River corridor for over 300 years, and the beauty of its diverse natural landscape and mildness of its climate have long been attractions. Maintaining that quality of life in this region, while preserving the natural diversity that directly contributes to it, is of primary concern to The Nature Conservancy in New York State.

The Conservancy has been working toward that end virtually since its inception. Its initial project and first donated property are both located in Westchester County, and its first chapter, the Eastern New York Chapter, was sanctioned in 1954. Today the region has two chapters, Eastern New York and Lower Hudson, which together manage over 10,000 acres (as of this writing) and have helped protect many more through voluntary agreements with independent landowners.

Along with over 150 other organizations dedicated to protecting the Hudson River, the Conservancy's focus has been to direct the resources of conservation partners toward protecting sites of high priority, such as Mill Creek Marsh in Columbia County. Meanwhile, the Conservancy has broadened its effort to encompass all that the region has to offer. This means the organization is increasingly working to preserve entire ecosystems such as the Neversink River watershed and the Shawangunk Mountains (the "Gunks")—two areas the Conservancy has designated as "Last Great Places." These protection efforts are designed to ensure that "quality of life" includes all the ingredients of that composite: biodiversity, natural beauty, and compatible human activities.

11 Mianus River Gorge Wildlife Refuge and Botanical Preserve

BEDFORD, WESTCHESTER COUNTY

555.20 ACRES

 The Mianus River Gorge is the "birthplace" of The Nature Conservancy's method of direct-action conservation. This was the first project the fledgling Conservancy became involved in when a group of local citizens came together to protect the gorge. Formed in 1953, the Mianus River Gorge Conservation Committee fostered the pioneer land preservation project of the Conservancy, and over 50 transactions have since added to the preserve's size. The Mianus River Gorge was registered as a National Natural Historic Landmark in 1964, the first natural area to be so designated.

The Mianus River, which begins in Greenwich, Connecticut, flows north through North Castle, New York, before reversing its course in Bedford and flowing south through the gorge and on into Long Island Sound. The river was named for Sachem Mayano of the Wappinger tribe, who was killed near the gorge in 1664, and whose name means "he who gathers together" in the Wappinger language. The gorge was likely formed by the waters of the receding Continental Ice Sheet 10,000 to 15,000 years ago. Other im-

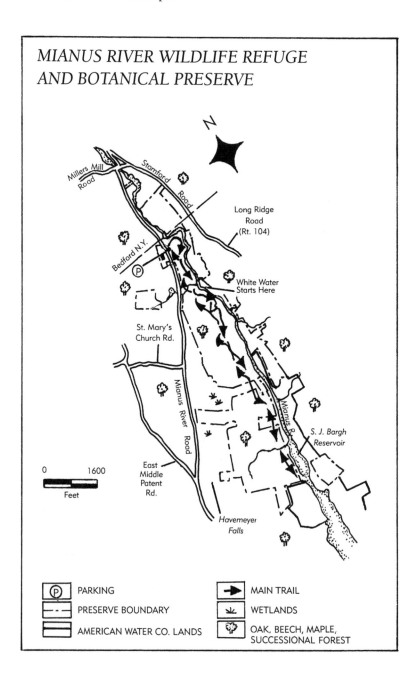

MIANUS RIVER WILDLIFE REFUGE AND BOTANICAL PRESERVE

Millers Mill Road

Stamford Road

Long Ridge Road (Rt. 104)

Bedford N.Y.

P

White Water Starts Here

St. Mary's Church Rd.

Mianus River Road

S. J. Bargh Reservoir

0   1600

Feet

East Middle Patent Rd.

Havemeyer Falls

PARKING

PRESERVE BOUNDARY

AMERICAN WATER CO. LANDS

MAIN TRAIL

WETLANDS

OAK, BEECH, MAPLE, SUCCESSIONAL FOREST

portant formations created by this glacial movement through what is now New York State include the Finger Lakes and Genesee Gorge upstate, the "potholes" of the Bronx River, and the mica schist found in New York City's Central Park.

There are three trails leading from the trail map at the shelter, and they represent varying distances and hiking times. We have found that the best way to see what the gorge has to offer is to walk a combination of the three trails, and that is what is described here.

Follow the Red (or Brink of Gorge) Trail, which begins to the left of the trail map and shelter. You will soon pass the Lucy Adams Memorial Bench, as well as an old field, and cross the Edith Faile Footbridge. At about the 0.25–mile mark the Bank of River Trail (blazed with white disks) will be to your left. This trail leads down to the riverbank at one of its narrowest stretches, and to the "Streamside Study Area," a place often used by scout troops and other groups as an outdoor classroom. Follow the white disks up past the Safford Cascade to rejoin the Red Trail at Point A. You are now 0.5 mile from the start of the trail and, if you choose to turn back, you can follow the Blue (Return) Trail back to the parking lot at this juncture. If you continue on the Red Trail, you will soon come to the Rockwall Breach, the narrowest point in the gorge, which was almost certainly cut by heavy glacial activity. Proceed a bit further and you will be standing in what is known as a hemlock cathedral. As of this writing, the grove is relatively untouched by the woolly adelgid aphid that has been the scourge of the once vast hemlock forests of the northeast. Some of these trees are well over 325 years old.

The cool, moist microclimate of the gorge provides an ideal environment for the growth of this hemlock–northern hardwood forest community of eastern hemlock (*Tsuga canadensis*), oak (*Quercus* sp.), and American beech (*Fagus grandifolia*) that is usually found in areas further north. There are also fine examples of a

Hiker at Mianus River Gorge

variety of other plants, including juniper (*Juniperus communis*), yellow birch (*Betula alleghanensis*), flowering dogwood (*Cornus florida*), and highbush blueberry (*Vaccinium corymbosum*). Much of the land surrounding the ravine itself was too steep to be of use to farmers, and as a result we have an impressive number of hundred-year-old trees here.

From Point B (at the 0.75-mile mark) you may also pick up

the Return Trail, but you will miss the impressive views of the S.J. Bargh Reservoir and Havemeyer Falls. There is also a side trail shortly after Point B, which leads to the Hobby Hill Quarry, where mica, quartz, and feldspar were mined out of the Bedford augen gneiss in the 18th century. Upon entering this quarry you will be dazzled by the exposed white and pink quartz. Please do not disturb or collect any of this quartz, but leave it for others to enjoy. The Bedford augen gneiss at Mianus River Gorge is generally assumed to be of Precambrian or early Paleozoic origin. Geologists estimate that the pegmatite, which intrudes into the gneiss, is around 375 million years old. The gneiss found here must be considerably older than the intruding pegmatite.

Continue on the Red Trail, following it past the Royal Fern Glen until you reach a side trail leading to the Reservoir View. Return to the Red Trail and continue to the next lookout. This is Havemeyer Falls. Be careful to follow the instructions on this trail, because serious erosion has caused the trail to be rerouted. Depending on when you visit the gorge, Havemeyer Falls can be an impressive, albeit gentle, cascade or a dry series of steps that ultimately lead to the reservoir. Back on the Red Trail, follow the trail to the shores of the reservoir and Point C.

Here you are likely to see bullfrogs (*Rana catesbeiana*), Fowler's toads (*Bufo woodhousei fowleri*), green frogs (*Rana clamitans*), and eastern painted turtles (*Chrysemys picta picta*). Return along the Blue Trail (much of which conjoins the Red Trail) back to the parking lot. Along the way you will pass through two fern glens: one of which, already mentioned, consists largely of royal ferns (*Osmunda regalis*) and occurs less than a quarter of the way along your return trip; the other is near the end of the trail. Over 30 species of ferns have been identified in the gorge, including hay-scented (*Dennstaedtia punctilobula*), New York (*Thelypteris noveboracensis*), and bulblet or bladder ferns (*Cystopteris bulbifera*). The entire walk takes about 2 hours.

VANISHING SONGBIRDS

Of all the birds breeding in northeastern forests, songbirds are perhaps the most notable and noticeable. Between 60 and 80 percent of these birds are neotropical migrant species. Each spring, their return heralds the lengthening of the days and the uplifting of our spirits. Recently, however, the steep decline in numbers of these migratory birds has been more noteworthy than their annual appearance.

The cerulean warbler (*Dendroica cerulea*), for instance, has decreased in the northeast by more than 60 percent since 1960. Still other species have become extirpated or locally extinct throughout their range. The cause of these declines is complex and not entirely understood, but there are a number of identifiable factors, including habitat destruction in the tropics and fragmentation of the landscape along songbirds' migratory routes and in their breeding areas.

Migrating songbirds move across North America at night in broad bands, taking advantage of tailwinds whenever possible. At dawn, they seek out suitable habitat in which to refuel, rest, and take shelter from hungry predators. The existence of stopover habitats is especially important adjacent to ecological barriers—vast areas where little or no bird habitat exists, such as most urban areas and large bodies of water. In New York, research by The Nature Conservancy and the New York Natural Heritage Program has documented concentrations of weary migratory birds in Lake Ontario's coastal forests and elsewhere. As migration "refueling stations" disappear or shrink in size and proportion, it becomes increasingly difficult for birds to consume enough to carry them to their destination.

The fragmentation of suitable feeding habitat along the birds' migratory routes can have a devastating effect on bird populations. This, along with the exposure to predation and parasitism in their breeding grounds and loss of winter habitat, leads to a dramatic decline in their numbers and in the quality of our lives here in the northeast. As a result, preservation of natural areas in the northeast is of increasing importance: Without the joyous sounds of songbirds each spring, what is left to wake us from our winter doldrums?

ACQUISITION

In 1953, the Mianus River Gorge Committee was formed to protect the gorge, and approximately 70 transactions have since added to the preserve's size.

DIRECTIONS

From NY 22, turn onto NY 172 east at the triangular green in Bedford Village. Proceed 0.8 mile and take the second right at the traffic light onto Long Ridge (Stamford) Road. Go 0.5 mile and turn right onto Miller's Mill Road. Proceed 0.1 mile over the bridge and turn left onto Mianus River Road. The entrance sign is 0.6 mile further on the left. (Lower Hudson Chapter)

ARTHUR W. BUTLER MEMORIAL SANCTUARY

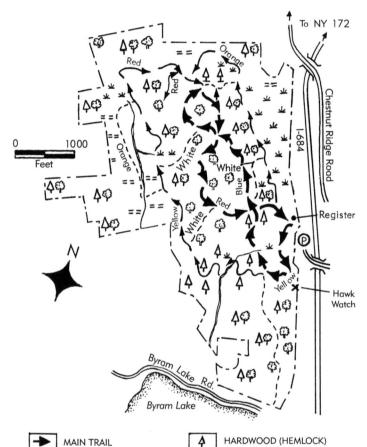

To NY 172

Chestnut Ridge Road

I-684

Red

Orange

Red

Orange

White

White

Blue

Red

Yellow

White

Red

Yellow

Register

Hawk Watch

Byram Lake Rd.

Byram Lake

0   1000
Feet

N

	MAIN TRAIL			HARDWOOD (HEMLOCK)
	SECONDARY TRAIL			OPEN FIELD
Ⓟ	PARKING			MIXED UPLAND FOREST
	PRESERVE BOUNDARY			HEMLOCK
	OAK, HICKORY			WETLANDS

12 *Arthur W. Butler Memorial Sanctuary*

MOUNT KISCO, WESTCHESTER COUNTY
371.47 ACRES

 While the Mianus River Gorge was the first project The Nature Conservancy became involved with, Butler Sanctuary was the first preserve donated to the fledgling organization. The land that comprises Butler was first acquired from the local Native Americans in 1700. Reporting in his "Record of the West Purchase, 1700–1740," John Copp found it "exceedingly rough, hilly mountainous, rockey [sic] and for the most part mean and unprofitable land." Walking through the sanctuary today, we must certainly agree that it is more suited for its current use as, in the words of Mrs. Butler, a "refuge for plants and wildlife and a living museum for man's use." Still, there are many indications that the early inhabitants of this part of New York attempted to wrest a livelihood from its "unprofitable" nature. Over 20 miles of stone walls crisscross the sanctuary, denoting grazing land and woodlots that were utilized at least until the early part of the current century.

The steep, rocky outcroppings occur on two ridges that run

PHOTOGRAPH © JOEL B. DYER 1990

Butler Sanctuary

in a north-south direction through the preserve. One of these, accentuated by the I-684 road cut, provides a perfect overlook from which to observe migrating hawks. The highest point of either ridge is 775 feet above sea level, and it is near here that the Robert J. Hamerschlag Hawkwatch was built in 1979. The hawkwatch, which at the time of this writing is undergoing a major renovation, is a cooperative venture between the Bedford and Greenwich Audubon Societies and The Nature Conservancy. In a typical year over 15,000 hawks are counted here, including broad-winged (*Buteo platypterus platypterus*) and sharp-shinned hawks (*Accipiter striatus velox*), Cooper's hawks (*Accipiter cooperii*), and peregrine falcons (*Falco peregrinus*).

Much of the sanctuary is dominated by upland deciduous forest, but it also contains a 30-acre red maple–hardwood swamp, a few successional old fields, and Broad Brook, which feeds the adjacent Byram Lake Reservoir and provides water for the village of Mount Kisco. This mix of habitat provides a safe haven for the uncommon, but relatively secure, spotted salamanders (*Ambystoma maculatum*).

The best way to see the Butler Sanctuary is to begin on the Yellow Trail and follow it up to the hawkwatch. Continue on the Yellow Trail to the edge of a coniferous forest, where the Yellow and Blue Trails meet. Take a right onto the Blue Trail and follow it through the mixed hardwoods/upland forest, crossing the Red Trail twice. You will loop around to the Red Trail a third time and here you should turn right onto it. The Red Trail will bring you back around in a figure eight and eventually out to the trail register and parking area. This trip will take between 1 and 2 hours, depending upon pace and time spent at the hawkwatch.

For those seeking a longer, more challenging hike, follow the Yellow Trail from the hawkwatch through the coniferous forest and up to the northwest corner of the sanctuary, where it meets the Red Trail. Follow the Red Trail until you reach a small successional old field on your left; make a left onto the Orange Trail. It will border the red maple swamp before emptying out onto the Red Trail near the main entrance. This loop takes an additional 3 to 4 hours, depending upon your pace.

ACQUISITION

The original 229 acres of Butler Sanctuary were given to the Conservancy in 1954 by Mrs. Arthur W. Butler, in memory of her husband. Additional acreage has been acquired over the years to expand the sanctuary to its current size.

DIRECTIONS:

From exit 4 off of I-684, go west on NY 172 toward Mount Kisco. After 0.3 mile turn left onto Chestnut Ridge Road. Proceed 1.2 miles and turn right onto the next bridge crossing over I-684. Park on the left near The Nature Conservancy preserve entrance sign. (Lower Hudson Chapter)

PAWLING NATURE RESERVE

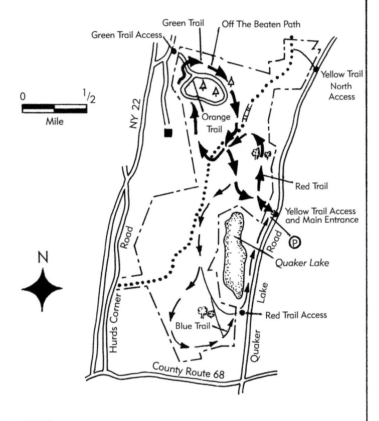

Green Trail Access

Green Trail

Off The Beaten Path

Yellow Trail North Access

NY 22

Orange Trail

Red Maple - Azalea Swamp

Red Trail

Yellow Trail Access and Main Entrance

Quaker Lake

Hurds Corner Road

Blue Trail

Red Trail Access

Quaker Lake Road

County Route 68

0   1/2
Mile

N

PRESERVE BOUNDARY

PARKING

MAIN TRAIL

BOARDWALK

APPALACHIAN TRAIL

HEMLOCK FOREST

RED MAPLE - AZALEA SWAMP

OPTIONAL TRAIL (EXTENSION)

VIEW SHED

13 *Pawling Nature Reserve*

PAWLING, DUCHESS COUNTY
1049.70 ACRES

 Much of the Pawling Nature Reserve is covered with second-growth oak woodlands, but among the other natural communities here are red maple–hardwood swamps, successional old fields, and, where several ravines allow for cooler microclimates, hemlock–northern hardwood forests, commonly known as "hemlock cathedrals." The reserve is part of the watershed of the Great Swamp, the second largest freshwater wetland in New York (after the Montezuma National Wildlife Refuge).

The single most important factor in determining the diversity of natural communities at the Pawling Reserve is Hammersly Ridge. This 1053-foot ridge runs north-south and not only provides some impressive views, but also affects the drainage of the surrounding areas. This topography allows for an unusual balance of ecosystems and causes such extreme differences in habitat that a xeric (dry) ridgetop of chestnut oak forest can grow within 30 feet of a red maple–hardwood swamp.

Chestnut oak forests, such as these on ridgetops, depend on very shallow soils with rapid drainage and little water retention. The dominant species is, as the name implies, chestnut oak (*Quer-*

cus montana), but the natural community includes red maple (*Acer rubrum*), scarlet oak (*Q. coccinea*), and pignut hickory (*Carya glabra*). Serviceberry (*Amelanchier canadensis*), scrub oak (*Q. ilicifolia*), and blueberry (*Vaccinium* sp.) also proliferate under the canopy of taller trees, along with wintergreen (*Gaultheria procumbens*) and trailing arbutus (*Epigaea repens*). Mountain laurel (*Kalmia latifolia*) forms a fringe around the slopes of this type of ridge, which you can quickly spy from the Red Trail along the easternmost edge of the preserve, north of Quaker Lake.

Logging and farming both have long histories on these lands. Sheep and cattle grazed here as early as 1750 and the fields were hayed as recently as the 1970s. The fields have recovered quickly, and today the woods and fields form a distinctive mosaic pattern. Remnants of human activity are everywhere: Not too far from the main entrance and trailhead for the Yellow Trail are the remains of a logging sluiceway and holding pond along Duell Hollow Brook. Foundations and stone walls provide further evidence of the historical use of this land.

The trail system at Pawling Reserve is quite extensive, and includes the Appalachian Trail (AT), the most frequently used trail at the reserve. About four people a day pass through the reserve via the AT, with more on weekends. Additional trails give a range of hiking experiences of varying lengths. The course we have chosen takes about 2 hours at a leisurely pace, but you could easily spend all day roaming around the reserve's other routes.

Enter the reserve from the main entrance along Quaker Lake Road, immediately north of Quaker Lake itself. On the Yellow Trail you will cross the sluiceway and Duell Hollow Brook before entering one of the reserve's hemlock cathedrals. This one rims the gorge, which was cut by the brook that cascades through it about 50 vertical feet. It follows a steeply sloped wooded ravine parallel to Quaker Lake Road.

There is some dispute over the status of hemlock-hardwood

Pawling Nature Reserve

forests as a climax community. A study completed in the Catskills in 1962 determined that hemlock is a transitional species, while a 1979 study at lower elevations in New Hampshire equated hemlocks with other climax species. What is the true status of hemlock-hardwood forests? Do they denote a forest in flux, or one that has already stabilized? The Pawling Nature Reserve is a prime place to examine both sides of the argument because it shares latitude with the Catskills and elevation with the site of the New Hampshire study.

From the gorge take a right (north) onto the Red Trail and follow it until you reach the boardwalk, where the trail joins the AT. You will want to take a left onto the AT/Red Trail and proceed in a southwesterly direction through an interconnected series of red maple–hardwood swamps that forms the largest example of this natural community in the reserve. After a little over 0.5 mile you will reach the Green Trail, at which point you should turn right (north). This portion of your journey takes you through the red maple–hardwood swamp that is in such curious proximity to one of the reserve's chestnut oak forests. The grade steepens slightly when you head west on the Orange Trail, but it is worth the climb for the view obtained from the ridgetop.

Follow the Orange Trail, bearing left at a fork about 0.25 mile from the overlook until it meets the Green Trail, which begins to head east and south. Portions of this trail can be difficult to decipher during late spring and early summer, as the green blazes blend with the surrounding foliage. At the point where the Green Trail intersects with the AT/Red Trail, take a right (south). What you are following is a figure eight that will ultimately lead back to the Yellow Trail Access (which is also the main entrance), and this part of the trail should be familiar since you have traveled it earlier in this walk. Bear left where the AT and Red Trails diverge and follow the AT until it forks with the Yellow Trail. Once on the Yellow Trail you are on the home stretch.

This is, as previously noted, about a 2-hour hike. If you prefer a longer loop, we suggest continuing on the AT for about 0.5 mile after the Yellow Trail/AT fork. Once again pick up the Red Trail and proceed south along it until you see blazes indicating the Blue Trail. This trail will take you around the southernmost extension of the reserve, which includes some steep (35 percent) grades and a plateau, before it exits at the Red Trail Access, south of Quaker Lake. From here you should walk north approximately 0.75 mile back to the main entrance. Leave yourself plenty of time for this longer loop—it makes for a good all-day excursion.

ACQUISITION

1015 acres were donated by the Akin Hall Association (Quaker Lake Corporation), a group of concerned local citizens, in 1958. 34.70 acres were acquired in 1983 from the Thomas Estate.

DIRECTIONS

Traveling north on NY 22, continue past the fork where NY 55 joins NY 22 from the west. Turn right at Hurds Corners Road (County Route 68) and proceed approximately 1 mile, bearing left (north) onto Quaker Lake Road. Follow this road 1.4 miles to the main entrance/parking area on your left. (Lower Hudson Chapter)

THOMPSON POND PRESERVE

0   800
Feet

N

Stissing Mt. Trail

To NY 199

Stissing Pond

Lake Road

To NY 82

Yellow Trail

Main Entrance

P

Register Box

Study Area

Blue Trail

Thompson Pond

Stissing Mt.

Wappingers Creek

MAIN TRAIL
SECONDARY TRAIL
BOARDWALK
WOODED HILL
FIRE TOWER
BEDROCK CLIFF
SIGN
EMERGENT MARSH

WOODED SWAMP
VERNAL POOL
PRESERVE BOUNDARY
OAK, HICKORY, BIRCH, MAPLE
CONIFERS
SWAMP

14 *Thompson Pond Preserve*

PINE PLAINS, DUCHESS COUNTY
372.63 ACRES

 The Thompson Pond basin was formed roughly 15,000 years ago at the end of the Pleistocene epoch, when a massive chunk of ice slowly melted to form a huge, irregularly shaped kettle. Through the deposition of sediments and the growth of marshlands, the kettle was divided into an interconnected chain of three bodies of water: Twin Island Lake (Mud Pond), Stissing Pond, and the half-mile-long Thompson Pond.

The area surrounding Thompson Pond is an excellent site for bird-watching, and perhaps the best location for water birds in the entire central Hudson valley region, with the possible exception of some points along the Hudson River itself. Thompson Pond also provides a stopover for warblers and other migrating birds, as well as nesting habitat for red-tailed hawks (*Buteo jamaicensis*), on nearby Stissing Mountain. The pond lies at the foot of the mountain and forms the origin of Wappingers Creek, which travels west and enters the Hudson at New Hamburg.

The 1403-foot Stissing Mountain is composed of Precambrian gneiss, while the younger lowlands are underlaid with limestone, shale, and slate. The "high stony hill good for little," described in

PHOTOGRAPH © ELLEN M. RAMSEY 1990

Thompson Pond Preserve

1743 by surveyor Charles Clinton, was later logged for charcoal, stripping the land of its original forests. Once the forests disappeared, however, so did the charcoal business. The new forest, as we see it today, consists of hardwoods, pines, and hemlocks. The unspoiled nature of Stissing was challenged again when Franklin D. Roosevelt, a frequent visitor to the Thompson Pond area from his Hyde Park estate, suggested that the Taconic State Parkway be extended to follow along the ridge. While this project would have enhanced the scenic quality of the highway, the ridge would surely have been destroyed as a result. Thankfully, the plan never left the drawing board.

The Conservancy came into the picture in 1957, when a committee of local citizens expressed concern for the preservation of Thompson Pond as a bird sanctuary and natural area. A local committee oversees the management of the preserve to this day, in conjunction with the Conservancy.

The beauty of this area has long been appreciated. Isaac Huntting, the principal historian of the region, noted that the area around Stissing Mountain "is a beautiful gem of creation . . . an altar in a grand unwalled temple of nature, where the soul finds joy and inspiration." A number of school and youth groups use this "beautiful gem" as an education center. The American Museum of Natural History devoted a large section of its Warburg Hall to the area, including a magnificent diorama of Stissing Mountain and the ponds. Thompson Pond itself became a registered National Natural Landmark in 1973.

Enter the Thompson Pond Preserve on the Yellow Trail at the parking area on Lake Road. Follow this trail through hardwoods and hemlocks, and its understory of hay-scented ferns (*Dennstaedtia punctilobula*). Thompson Pond will be to your left and you can see Stissing Mountain up above the trees off to your right. If you want a closer look at the pond, take a left onto the Blue Trail and loop back around to the Yellow Trail, which leads through another stand of hemlock.

After the hemlock, you will come to a knoll that looks out over the pond and then descends to the water's edge. This is all that remains of the "wall" of the original kettle lake; glacial outwash carried most of it away and the rest is buried deep beneath thousands of years of soil buildup. Around a cove from the wall lies a red maple–hardwood swamp. This type of swamp community consists of red maple (*Acer rubrum*), sweet pepperbush (*Clethra alnifolia*), Canada mayflower (*Maianthemum canadense*), and sphagnum moss (*Sphagnum* sp.). The trail then continues along the kettle bank, until it takes a sharp left at the edge of a farm field. If you keep the field on your right you will soon come to a boardwalk through the swamp. A second boardwalk will reveal more pastureland and fields, and a third will cross Wappingers Creek at the very beginning of its 30-mile trek to the Hudson. Follow the trail up a knoll to an open field and then uphill past an eastern hophornbeam (*Ostrya virginiana*), which has interesting hoplike scales around its nuts, making the fruit look like it is enclosed in tiny paper bags. Shortly after this tree the trail follows along a fence lined by blackberries (*Rubus* spp.), and into a small stand of tall imported Norway spruce (*Picea abies*). You will then come to Lake Road, at which you should turn left and proceed back to the parking area. This loop takes approximately 2 hours.

For an overview of the Stissing Mountain area, you may want to visit the fire tower on Stissing's northern slope. From the parking area, take Lake Road north approximately 1500 feet to the trailhead on your left (look for the Yellow Trail marker). Follow the trail until you reach a fork; take the right fork and then bear left (south) at each ensuing fork until you reach the fire tower.

The fire tower stands on an acre of land that the Conservancy recently transferred to the Friends of Stissing Landmarks (FOSL), a local group devoted to protecting and maintaining landmarks in the area. FOSL maintains the fire tower for public access. From this vantage point you will be able to see both Stissing Pond and Twin Island Lake, although Thompson Pond will be hidden from view except when the trees are bare.

Continue on the trail in a north-northwesterly direction down the mountain and back to Lake Road. This trip takes 1 hour, depending upon your pace.

ACQUISITION

The initial purchase of 173.58 acres was made by a local committee in 1958, with additional acreage purchased in 1973, 1988, and 1989.

DIRECTIONS

From the Taconic State Parkway take the US 44 exit. Go 0.5 mile toward Millbrook, then take NY 82 North for about 15 miles. At Pine Plains fire house turn left onto Lake Road and proceed 1.6 miles. The entrance to the preserve is on the left, at the foot of Stissing Mountain. Cars may be parked on the roadside. (Lower Hudson Chapter)

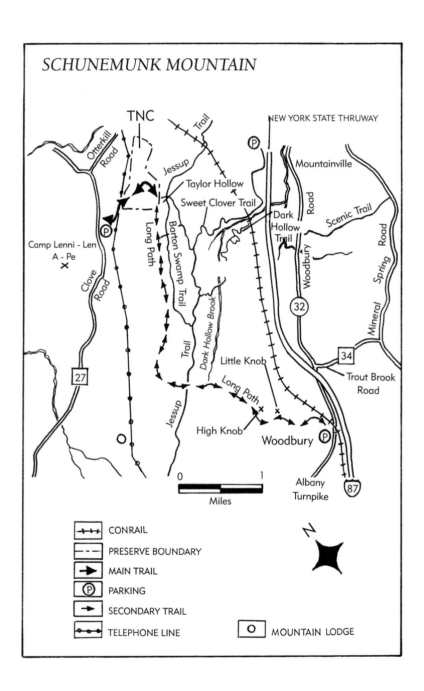

SCHUNEMUNK MOUNTAIN

TNC

Jessup Trail

NEW YORK STATE THRUWAY

Otterkill Road

Mountainville

Taylor Hollow

Sweet Clover Trail

Dark Hollow Trail

Scenic Trail

Jessup

Long Path

Barton Swamp Trail

Camp Lenni - Len A - Pe

Clove Road

Woodbury Road

Mineral Spring Road

Dark Hollow Brook

Little Knob

Jessup Trail

Long Path

High Knob

Trout Brook Road

Woodbury

Albany Turnpike

0   1
Miles

CONRAIL

PRESERVE BOUNDARY

MAIN TRAIL

Ⓟ PARKING

SECONDARY TRAIL

TELEPHONE LINE

Ⓞ MOUNTAIN LODGE

N

15 Schunemunk Mountain

ORANGE COUNTY
163.24 ACRES

 In the northern Hudson Highlands, an 8-mile long, north-south running ridge called Schunemunk Mountain rises 1625 feet above the Hudson River valley. An Algonquin (Lenape) word meaning "excellent fireplace," Schunemunk (pronounced SKUN-uh-munk), has some stunning views and a geologic structure that is remarkably different than that commonly associated with the Highlands. It is, in fact, much younger, being a combination of strata from Devonian (395–345 million years old), Silurian (435–395 million years old), and Ordovician (500–435 million years old) eras.

The ridge was formed as an ancient sea drained with the rise of the Taconic Highlands to the east, which in turn was caused by the collision of the European and North American continents. The two ridges then folded into one another—imagine two giant shoulders coming together in an affectionate embrace and you can visualize this geologic event.

A trail system maintained by the New York–New Jersey Trail Conference traverses Schunemunk Mountain. This system includes the Long Path, upon which you can travel from New York

City's George Washington Bridge to the Catskills. The Long Path actually crosses The Nature Conservancy's preserve on Schunemunk, and represents the only marked trail on the 163-acre preserve at the northwest corner of the ridge.

The Schunemunk Mountain Preserve harbors an excellent example of the natural community known as chestnut oak forest. This is a hardwood forest dominated by chestnut oak (*Quercus montana*) and red oak (*Quercus rubra*). American chestnut (*Castanea dentata*) was a common associate in these forests prior to the chestnut blight, and chestnut sprouts can still be found in some stands, although they do not mature. Characteristic shrubs include black huckleberry (*Gaylussacia baccata*) and mountain laurel (*Kalmia latifolia*), and common groundlayer plants are Pennsylvania sedge (*Carex pensylvanica*), wild sarsaparilla (*Aralia nudicaulis*), wintergreen (*Gaultheria procumbens*), and cushions of the aptly named white cushion moss (*Leucobryum glaucum*).

A New York State–rare natural community found on Schunemunk is pitch pine–oak–heath rocky summit, which usually occurs on warm, dry ridgetops. It is sparsely vegetated, with pitch pine (*Pinus rigida*) and chestnut oak forming a canopy over blueberries (*Vaccinium* spp.), sweet-fern (*Comptonia peregrina*), and poverty grass (*Danthonia spicata*), along with lichens such as Iceland moss (*Cetraria arenaria*) and *Cladonia* sp.

Schunemunk has the distinction of being one of the last known habitats in New York State for the Allegheny or eastern woodrat (*Neotoma floridana*), which is now likely extirpated in the state. Recently, three rare moths, *Catocala herodias gerhardi, Apharetra purpurea,* and *Itame species* have been reported on Schunemunk, although further research is needed to determine the extent of their presence. Until now, the only known New York State occurrence of *Catocala herodias gerhardi* was in the pine barrens of Long Island, and even there only 5 or 10 populations have been found. *Itame species* is a coastal and sandy pine barrens species that

PHOTOGRAPH © THE NATURE CONSERVANCY/OLIVIA MILLARD

Schunemunk Mountain

is sometimes found on ridgetops such as Schunemunk.

There are at least two ways to experience Schunemunk.

1. From the parking lot at the Hil Mar Inn on County Route 27 (Clove Road), north of Camp Lenni-Len-A-Pe, follow the Long Path (blue blazes) up to the Conservancy's preserve (at about 650 feet). This trail will take you up to 1300 feet after nearly 1.5 miles, and will leave the preserve where the Long Path, Jessup (yellow), and Barton Swamp (red) Trails converge. Return on the Long Path back to the parking area. This hike will take roughly 2 hours, depending upon your pace.

2. For a longer hike (approximately 12 miles round trip), you can enter the Long Path (blue blazes) from the parking lot near the railroad trestle on NY 32, in the town of Woodbury. Follow the Long Path northwest approximately 2.5 miles until it bears north-northeast shortly after crossing the yellow-blazed Jessup Trail, overlooking the Mountain Lodge housing development. About 3 miles further, the Long Path will join the red-blazed Barton Swamp Trail heading west-northwest into The Nature Conservancy's preserve site and eventually down to the parking lot at the Hil Mar Inn on County Route 27 (Clove Road). If you have two cars, it is a good idea to leave one here as well as in Woodbury. Otherwise, you will have to retrace your steps on the blue-blazed trail, or return along the red-blazed trail to Taylor Hollow and then join the yellow-blazed Jessup Trail southwest to the summit and back on the Long Path to Woodbury. This round-trip hike is approximately 12 miles, so be certain to get an early start and bring plenty of water.

ACQUISITION

This 163.24-acre piece of land was donated by Mrs. Mabel Ingalls in 1991.

DIRECTIONS

For Hike 1: Take US 6/NY 17 to exit 130 (NY 208); follow NY 208 north to County Route 27 (Clove Road). Continue on County Route 27 approximately 5.2 miles to the Hil Mar Inn. Park in the lot and hike to the Long Path trailhead (blue blazes).

For Hike 2: Take exit 16 (Harriman) from the New York State Thruway (I-87), then head north on NY 32 to Woodbury. Park in the parking lot near the railroad trestle and hike to the trailhead. There are also buses from the Port Authority Bus Terminal in Manhattan that go to Woodbury. (Lower Hudson Chapter)

NEVERSINK PRESERVE

0 — 500
Feet

Graham Road

BP — Blue
Blue
Beaver Swamp
BP
Register
Orange

BP
Red
White
White
Yellow
Neversink River
BP
BP

N

BP	BEAVER POND
P	PARKING
---	PRESERVE BOUNDARY
⊥	SWAMP
==	SUCCESSIONAL MIXED HARDWOODS / OLD FIELDS
)))	AGRICULTURAL FIELDS

FLOODPLAIN FOREST
MIXED HARDWOOD FOREST
CONIFEROUS FOREST
MAIN TRAIL

16 *Neversink Preserve*

DEERPARK, ORANGE COUNTY
206.06 ACRES

 Less than 2 hours from New York City, the Neversink is a pristine river originating on the slopes of Slide Mountain, the highest peak in the Catskill Mountains. Two main tributaries merge at the border of Ulster and Sullivan Counties, and the river slows, flowing southwest into the Neversink Reservoir. From there, it swiftly runs to the Neversink Gorge, where it is secluded for several miles between high walls, and then proceeds past villages and farms until it ultimately empties into the Delaware River in New Jersey.

This Lower Hudson Chapter preserve is home to the world's largest and healthiest population of the globally imperiled dwarf wedgemussel (*Alasmidonta heterodon*). Fewer than 20 populations of this mussel, which was listed as a federally endangered species in 1990, exist worldwide. Two other rare freshwater mussels have also been found in the lower Neversink, brook floater (*Alasmidonta varicosa*) and alewife floater (*Anodonta implicata*).

Because the Neversink's endangered mussels are found in the lowest reaches of the river, the Conservancy hopes to protect the entire watershed to ensure the good water quality necessary to

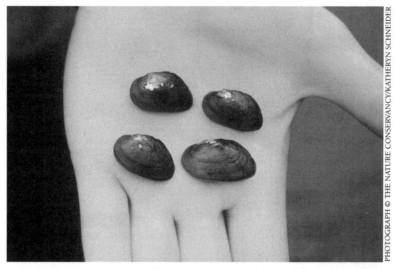

Dwarf wedgemussels (*Alasmidonta heterodon*)

PHOTOGRAPH © THE NATURE CONSERVANCY/KATHERYN SCHNEIDER

their survival. Water pollution and sedimentation have eliminated the dwarf wedgemussel from other drainages. During the juvenile stage, mussels depend on attachment to the gills of host fish, which disperse the mussels throughout the river. Although much research on freshwater mussels remains to be done, it is clear that they are important indicators of the overall health of a river system.

Maintaining the Neversink's water quality is also vital for people. The upper Neversink constitutes part of the New York City water supply system, and millions of people rely on the river for clean drinking water. In addition, the river is one of the finest fly-fishing streams on the eastern seaboard. Theodore Gordon established the sport in this country on the Neversink in the 1800s. Today, the river is still a haven for anglers and others who seek out clean waters abundant with a variety of fish.

The river also supports much of the native flora and fauna considered representative of inland Atlantic streams. There are at least 132 species of birds, 47 fish species, 17 reptile species, and

14 species of amphibians that inhabit the Neversink River watershed. Ospreys (*Pandion haliaetus carolinensis*), bald eagles (*Haliaeetus leucocephalus*), and two globally rare dragonflies have also been seen along the river. In addition, a concentration of limestone caves has been discovered, one of which contains five of the six bat species known to occur in New York State, including the globally rare small-footed bat (*Myotis leibii*). The preserve also includes a fine example of floodplain forests and fields that grow above the local aquifer.

In 1991, the US Fish and Wildlife Service published a Species Recovery Plan for the dwarf wedgemussel, in which the Neversink plays a critical role. Now, the Conservancy is contributing to this effort by devising a broad conservation strategy to protect not only the water quality of the river, but compatible economic activities that are vital to the area's human communities.

The unfolding strategy to preserve the watershed's integrity involves cooperative efforts with public and private agencies and landowners, specifically those that have the capacity to affect the river through land-use-related activities. Key concerns are the various sources of pollution and sedimentation resulting from agriculture, golf courses, water release from dams, and other development and activities.

Although considered pristine, the Neversink is no stranger to environmental threats. In the 1960s, the river's health was in serious jeopardy: New York City began pumping clean water from the upper reaches at the same time that resorts in the Catskills were releasing effluents into the lower river system. This severe problem has since been ameliorated through more stringent regulations, but in recent years the Neversink's integrity has been under pressure from the development of a landfill in Sullivan County. Landfill building activities have led to increased siltation in the river, and contaminated water leaching from the landfill is now a problem. Sand and gravel mining in the area compounds the problem of erosion into the river and current agricultural practices also pose a long-term threat.

With the help of hydrologists, soil scientists, engineers, and local residents, the Conservancy is now focusing efforts on research along the Neversink. Through these studies it hopes to learn more about the species of fish that serve as host to the dwarf wedgemussel, and the effects that an upstream dam might have on the mussel population. Research is needed to determine the environmental preferences of the mussel, the importance of sediment stability in regulating its distribution, and the exact current population size and geographical location of the species.

In addition, the Neversink River has been nominated as one of the Conservancy's Last Great Places. "Last Great Places: An Alliance for People and the Environment" is an ambitious conservation program designed to protect outstanding ecosystems in the United States, Latin America, and the Pacific. At each location, the Conservancy is working closely with partners, both public and private, to demonstrate that economic, recreational, and other development can occur while preserving nature.

From the trailhead near the parking area, follow the Blue Trail to your left through several successional old fields; bear left at each successive fork in the trail as it winds around a barn and crosses a small creek by means of a series of pontoon bridges. Once across the creek, you will enter the floodplain forest community. Bear left at the next fork and follow the trail to the riverbank. Take a right onto the Yellow Trail along the bank of the river, continuing through the floodplain along the river. There are a couple of nice resting spots along this stretch, where you can get a clear view of the Neversink. Continue on the Yellow Trail, taking a left where it intersects with the Red and White Trails, to the southernmost portion of the preserve, where the trail turns sharply to the right (west) and crosses the creek again over a bridge. Here the trail becomes the Orange Trail. Continue on the Orange Trail and bear left at each successive intersection. You will then enter another old field that leads back to the parking area. This loop takes between 1 and 2 hours, depending upon how much time you take by the river's edge.

ACQUISITION

In 1991, 36 acres were donated to The Nature Conservancy by Ogden, et al. An additional 170 acres were purchased in 1993.

DIRECTIONS

From NY 17 West take exit 113 (Wurtsboro/Ellenville); make a left off the ramp onto US 209 South (toward Port Jervis). Follow US 209 for approximately 9.5 miles, crossing the Neversink River over a steel bridge (notice the historic marker for the old D & H Canal). Once over the bridge, take the second left onto Old Route 209-3 (follow signs for the American Family Campground). Follow this road until it forks. Bear left and then take a left onto Graham Road. Proceed 200 yards; take a right onto a dirt road that leads to the preserve gate. You must obtain the combination to the lock from the chapter office (see appendix 2). Proceed along this road to the cul-de-sac parking area and follow the signs to the trailhead. (Lower Hudson Chapter)

LEWIS A. SWYER PRESERVE
AT MILL CREEK MARSH

0   1/4
Mile

N

Hudson River

Mill Creek

NY 9J

Pond

CANOE LAUNCH
MAIN TRAIL
MUDFLATS
SWAMP
BOARDWALK
BRIDGE
RAILROAD
OVERPASS
PRESERVE BOUNDARY
TEACHING PLATFORM
OBSERVATION TOWER

17 Lewis A. Swyer Preserve at Mill Creek Marsh

TOWN OF STUYVESANT, COLUMBIA COUNTY
95 ACRES
HANDICAPPED ACCESSIBLE

 Tidal wetlands once lined much of both banks of the Hudson River, which is tidal from New York City upstream to Troy, New York. The building of railroads and other industrial complexes, however, has impinged upon the natural interaction between river and shore, thereby disturbing the balance of some very delicate ecosystems. Today there are fewer than 10 occurrences of tidal wetlands along the Hudson River, and Mill Creek Marsh is one of only 5 freshwater tidal swamps in New York State.

The importance of wetlands cannot be overstressed. Not only are they aesthetically pleasing, wetlands are the "farmland" of our rivers, streams, and coasts. The organic energy generated by marshes and swamps is astounding, rivaling that of our most fertile croplands. Some marshes can produce over 10 tons of organic matter per unit size in a single year. The detritus, as the decaying and decomposing plant matter is called, becomes food for countless microorganisms. These become food for fish, which in turn

PHOTOGRAPH © THE NATURE CONSERVANCY

Boardwalk at Lewis A. Swyer Preserve

are important food resources for bird, mammal, and human populations. Wetlands can also help prevent damage from floods and storms, as well as improve water quality through a strict regulation of effluents and excess nutrients that pass into the wetlands from flooding waters and natural runoff.

The Lewis A. Swyer Preserve at Mill Creek Marsh actually contains four aquatic communities: a freshwater tidal swamp, a freshwater tidal marsh, freshwater intertidal mudflats, and a creek. Of these, the swamp is probably the most prominent. What is the difference between a marsh and a swamp? A marsh is an open wetland typically covered by about 6 inches of water. A swamp, on the other hand, is a wetland dominated by woody plants that is only saturated or flooded during wet seasons.

The type of swamp at this preserve is created by the relatively moderate grade of the Hudson, which allows the tidal waters easy access to the wetland.

Species growing in this forested swamp community include green ash (*Fraxinus pennsylvanica*), black ash (*F. nigra*), slippery elm (*Ulmus rubra*), and swamp white oak (*Quercus bicolor*). Shrubs you are likely to find here include spicebush (*Lindera benzoin*), arrowwood (*Viburnum recognitum*), and buttonbush (*Cephalanthus occidentalis*). Groundcover plants include rice cutgrass (*Leersia oryzoides*), sensitive fern (*Onoclea sensibilis*), swamp milkweed (*Asclepias incarnata*), and the ubiquitous skunk cabbage (*Symplocarpus foetidus*), along with Virginia creeper (*Parthenocissus quinquefolia*) and hog-peanut (*Amphicarpea bracteata*). Bald eagles (*Haliaeetus leucocephalus*) have been known to nest and winter along the river. They share the bountiful food of the wetlands with herons, ducks, and passerines, which also use the preserve.

Railroad tracks owned and operated by Conrail, and formerly by the New York–Penn Central railroad, unnaturally separate the swamp from the mudflats at the river's edge, preventing direct access to the shore. The Eastern New York Chapter of the Conservancy has included the Lewis A. Swyer Preserve in its Priority Lands Protection Program, an initiative designed to preserve the most endangered natural resources in Eastern New York. A half-mile-long boardwalk constructed by the chapter leads through the swamp, following the natural contours of Mill Creek. At the end of the boardwalk is an observation deck that affords a panoramic view of the Hudson. In addition, a canoe access to the river is located on Mill Creek, making the Swyer Preserve an excellent site from which to intimately experience the Hudson and its wetland communities. *Please note: You will be unable to access the canoe launch if you return when the tide is out. Check tidal times before your trip.* The boardwalk to the river and back takes about 30 minutes to walk, but allow for more time to observe the plants and animals from the deck. High water in the spring and late autumn occasionally covers the entire boardwalk. Flooding is greatest during storms at or near the occurrence of a full moon.

ACQUISITION

Purchased in 1989, this land is named in honor of Lewis A. Swyer, a former Eastern New York Chapter Trustee.

DIRECTIONS

From Albany, take US 9 and US 20 to Rensselaer, turn right (south) onto NY 9J and continue through the Village of Castleton. Approximately 7.7 miles beyond Castleton, you will pass under a railroad bridge. The parking lot is located about 0.5 mile from the railroad bridge on the right side of NY 9J. The trail entrance is about 500 feet down the road just before a bridge that crosses Mill Creek. (Eastern New York Chapter)

18 *Albany Pine Bush*

ALBANY, ALBANY COUNTY

991.16 ACRES (acquired by The Nature Conservancy; or Conservancy-assisted acquisitions)

 Like many of New York's natural areas, the Albany Pine Bush, home of the federally endangered Karner blue butterfly (*Lycaeides melissa samuelis*), was formed in the wake of a retreating glacier some 15,000 years ago. The glacier left behind a series of lakes, including glacial Lake Albany, which once stretched from present-day Glens Falls to Newburgh, and from Albany to Schenectady.

When Lake Albany drained, it left behind huge deposits of sand and gravel, which prevailing winds formed into large dunes. Because the dunes were porous and lacking in nutrients, plants could not quickly colonize and stabilize the sand. When the dune-stabilizing plants finally began to populate the sandy soils, they eventually formed a natural community known as pitch pine–scrub oak barrens.

Fires are a necessary component of this type of community, and are known to occur in a 6- to 12-year cycle. As with other pine barren communities described in this book, the Albany Pine Bush consists mainly of scrub oaks (*Quercus ilicifolia* and *Q. prinoides*),

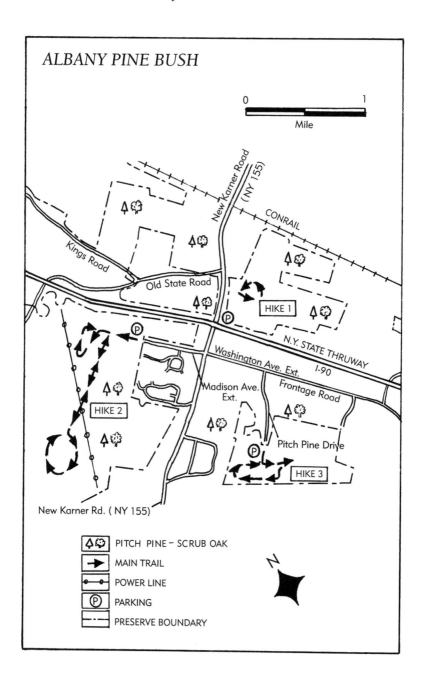

ALBANY PINE BUSH

pitch pine (*Pinus rigida*), and plants that are adapted to frequent fires. Pitch pine has fire-resistant bark and can actually sprout new growth relatively soon after fire has subsided. Its cones use fire to open and disperse their seeds. Scrub oak, on the other hand, defends against fire by storing the energy needed to develop new growth deep within its root systems. Invasive trees like quaking aspen (*Populus tremuloides*) and black cherry (*Prunus serotina*), which are among the first trees to colonize a disturbed area, cannot defend against fire; when fire is suppressed, these species quickly take over the pine barrens community, transforming it into a typical Eastern deciduous forest.

Along with pitch pine and scrub oaks, you will notice a number of smaller plants that thrive in this type of environment. These include big and little bluestem grass (*Andropogon gerardii* and *Schizachyrium scoparium*), sweet-fern (*Comptonia peregrina*), blueberry (*Vaccinium* sp.), black huckleberry (*Gaylussacia baccata*), bush-clover (*Lespedeza capitata*), goat's-rue (*Tephrosia virginiana*), and wild lupine (*Lupinus perennis*).

Wild lupine is the food of choice for the Karner blue butterfly during its caterpillar stage. The iridescent blue wings, with orange spots on the underside of its rear wings, make the Karner blue a joy to see. Look for them in late May–early June and again in late July–early August, when they emerge from their cocoons.

The fragmentation of the Albany Pine Bush has resulted in drastically reduced numbers of the Karner blues over the last 10 years. Of course, this habitat fragmentation is nothing new. As late as the 17th century, the Pine Bush spread over 40 square miles in the upper Hudson River valley. The arrival of European settlers, the use of the abundant pine in the construction of Fort Orange, and the mining of the sand dunes for the Hudson's many iron foundries established a pattern of dissection for this distinctive natural area. Roads and highways began to appear in the 19th century, and continued to expand and encroach with the growth of the city of Albany and its suburbs throughout the current century. The pine barrens have been decimated; it is estimated that of the original 25,600 acres, a mere 3000 acres remain.

To stem the destruction of this valuable resource, the Albany Pine Bush Commission (APBC) was established by the New York State Legislature in 1988. The Commission is charged with coordinating the effort to manage and protect the last remaining Pine Bush communities. The Conservancy participates on the Commission by acquiring land and partaking in a prescribed burning program. The burn program has restored the natural process that has been kept in check by fire suppression.

TNC and APBC are working to complete a reasonably contiguous preserve, which managed properly can be a viable community for the more than 156 species of birds, 30 mammal species, and numerous reptiles and amphibians who live there. The Eastern New York Chapter of the Conservancy has included the Albany Pine Bush in its Priority Lands Protection Program.

There are a number of trail systems available at the Albany Pine Bush, but for the purposes of this book we will describe three. The first is known as Karner Barrens East. From the Washington Avenue Extension west of Albany, turn right onto New Karner Road (NY 155) where you will notice a water tower. Proceed over the New York State Thruway (I-90), where you will see a parking area on your right directly after the overpass. Walk north along New Karner Road and look for the gate and sign near the State Employee Federal Credit Union building. The trail courses through the pitch pine–scrub oak barrens community and up to a dune from which you can obtain views of the Helderburg and Catskill Mountains. Retrace your steps back to the gate and parking area. This tour takes approximately 20 minutes.

If you would like to experience the largest inland sand dune in New York State, known as the Great Dune, follow the directions above, but do not turn at New Karner Road (NY 155); in-

PHOTOGRAPH © THE NATURE CONSERVANCY

Albany Pine Bush

stead go straight on the Madison Avenue Extension. Drive to the end of this road and park. Follow the trail that is directly ahead of you, then take a left at the first intersection in the trail. This trail continues under power lines and beyond a yellow gate. At the next left you will arrive at the base of the Great Dune. The U-shaped Great Dune is roughly 0.75 mile long; the trail will take you to the top of the dune and around its base. Retrace your steps back to the parking area. This walk takes about 1.5 hours.

Our favorite hike in the Pine Bush is called Blueberry Hill, and it is a medium-length hike, taking a little more than an hour. Once again, take the Washington Avenue Extension, but this time turn left at the third traffic light after Fuller Road (just beyond an Italian-American Community Center). Turn right immediately af-

THE GUNKS: A "LAST GREAT PLACE"

The northern Shawangunk Mountains are made of hard conglomerate sandstone created from braided streams that flowed more than 400 million years ago. At the core of the proposed Shawangunks Bioreserve, the northern Shawangunks contain five globally rare natural communities, the most important of which is the dwarf pine ridge community, an area of over 5000 acres of pitch pine (*Pinus rigida*). Although structurally similar to natural communities found in the Long Island and New Jersey pine barrens, the Shawangunks pine barrens are unique in that they exist at an elevation of 2000 feet. In addition, at least 11 rare species are present on the ridge.

The pitch pine found in the Shawangunks is some of the oldest in existence, with trees over 300 years old. Generally less than 6 to 10 feet tall, the dwarf pines have adapted to frequent fire and disturbance from wind and ice. It is believed that this fire-dependent community was formed approximately 2000 years ago during a period of global climate change. At the same time, Native Americans were developing permanent settlements and using fire as a means of clearing fields and manipulating the landscape.

The Eastern New York Chapter, in coordination with a number of public and private conservation interests in the Gunks, is focusing research and preservation efforts on the most fragile and threatened areas of ecological significance. In 1994, the chapter helped to establish and lead the Shawangunk Biodiversity Partnership, which has attracted the funding essential to research and management that will provide a better understanding of the intricate balance of natural communities there and the forces that maintain them.

ter this onto South Frontage Road. Then take the first left onto Pitch Pine Drive, proceed to the end, and park at the gate. The trail courses through a pitch pine–scrub oak community, ending at a T-junction. Take a left here onto the trail that ascends Blueberry Hill for a view of the Helderburgs. Retrace your steps back to the T-junction, where this time you will go straight (turning right will take you back to your car). This trail will take you on a loop that winds through the heart of the Albany Pine Bush, where you will gain a greater understanding of the threats to its integrity.

ACQUISITION

The Nature Conservancy purchased its first parcel in the Albany Pine Bush in 1984. The Conservancy has helped acquire additional acreage since that time, involving many state and local agencies. As of 1994, 2200 acres of the Albany Pine Bush have been protected by the Albany Pine Bush Commission, which includes The Nature Conservancy, the New York State Department of Environmental Conservation, the Office of Parks, Recreation and Historical Preservation, the City of Albany, the towns of Guilderland and Colonie, and three citizens.

DIRECTIONS

See trail descriptions above. (Eastern New York Chapter)

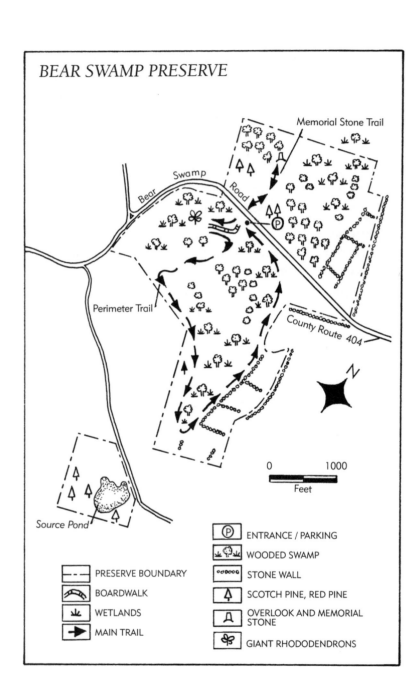

BEAR SWAMP PRESERVE

Memorial Stone Trail

Bear Swamp Road

Perimeter Trail

County Route 404

N

0   1000
Feet

Source Pond

⊕ ENTRANCE / PARKING

WOODED SWAMP

STONE WALL

SCOTCH PINE, RED PINE

OVERLOOK AND MEMORIAL STONE

GIANT RHODODENDRONS

PRESERVE BOUNDARY

BOARDWALK

WETLANDS

MAIN TRAIL

19 *Bear Swamp Preserve*

WESTERLO, ALBANY COUNTY
235.95 ACRES

 Two swamps called Little Bear and Big Bear make up this wetland complex and contain hundreds of giant rhododendron (*Rhododendron maximum*), which are more common in the Smoky Mountains of eastern Tennessee than in the northern Catskills. In fact, Bear Swamp Preserve represents one of the northernmost natural occurrences of these plants. They can survive here because of the high water table of the swamp, which protects the rhododendron roots during the long winter months.

The best time to see these plants in full flourish is from the end of June into early July, when their large white flowers cover the green foliage. Bog plants such as sphagnum moss (*Sphagnum* sp.), goldthread (*Coptis trifolia*), leatherleaf (*Chamaedaphne calyculata*), winterberry (*Ilex verticillata*), highbush blueberry (*Vaccinium corymbosum*), and Labrador tea (*Ledum groenlandicum*) are also found in the swamps.

Giant rhododendrons have an intricate network of trunks and branches. They are known to create such a tangled mess that southern mountaineers, surveying lands in the Smokies, often referred to stands of these bushes as "rhododendron hells." If you

Giant rhododendron (*Rhododendron maximum*) at Bear Swamp

PHOTOGRAPH BY SUSAN BOURNIQUE

visit Bear Swamp during the peak flowering of the rhododendrons, feel the sticky stems of the flowers. This natural protection prevents ants and flying insects from stealing the pollen and spreading it to other flowering plants. Although other species of rhododendrons are now quite common as ornamental plants, they did not actually become popular until after the 1876 Centennial Exhibition in Philadelphia.

In Big Bear Swamp, the sphagnum moss has been measured to a depth of over 20 feet, and carbon dating has revealed that it is about 13,000 years old. The two swamps are separated by a ledge of sandstone and there is no surface water connecting them.

The entrance to the preserve is marked by a large Conservancy sign on the south side of Bear Swamp Road. A loop to the south (the Perimeter Trail) will take you through part of Big Bear Swamp, but the best view of the giant rhododendron is had from a boardwalk that extends off to the right of the trailhead. The trail is relatively dry during the summer months; however, beaver (*Castor canadensis*) have been known to dam the outlet to the swamp, so wear waterproof boots just in case. The foliage along the loop can sometimes obscure the trail, so be prepared. Particularly striking are the large ferns—mostly cinnamon fern (*Osmunda cinnamomea*) and crested shield fern (*Dryopteris cristata*)—that crowd the boardwalk and trail.

An old lane to the north of Bear Swamp Road is lined with red pine (*Pinus resinosa*) and leads to Little Bear Swamp. At the end of the lane, where you can look out over the swamp, you will find a memorial stone dedicated to the local conservationists who helped establish this preserve.

Source Pond, also part of the preserve, is located about 0.75 mile south on a dirt road off of Bear Swamp Road. The pond is too shallow for fish, but does support a wide variety of bird life, including red-winged blackbirds (*Agelaius phoeniceus*), pileated woodpeckers (*Dryocopus pileatus*), goshawks (*Accipiter gentilis*), and 19 species of warblers.

This land was originally purchased by the Van Rensselaer family in 1629 and sold to a Mr. Bear in the late 1800s, hence the preserve's name. Throughout the United States, however, there are many "Bear Swamps" with similar vegetation (this may be one of the most prevalent geographical names after "Camel's Hump" and "Great Swamp"), which were probably so named because bears frequented the areas for the copious blueberries. The last bear sighting at this Bear Swamp occurred over 25 years ago. White-tailed deer (*Odocoileus virginianus*) *are* common browsers at Bear Swamp however. Look for evidence of their presence on the rhododendrons: there is a distinct lack of foliage below the 4-foot level. Retrace your steps back to Bear Swamp Road and to your car. The entire hike, including the boardwalk and the lane leading to Little Bear Swamp, takes between 1 and 2 hours.

ACQUISITION

The initial purchase was made in 1960, with additional acreage added in 1965, 1966, and 1984. Bear Swamp is a Registered Natural Landmark of the Department of the Interior.

DIRECTIONS

From the intersection of US 9W and NY 32 south of Albany, head southwest on NY 32 through the town of Feura Bush and across the Alcove Reservoir. Approximately 2 miles past the reservoir there is an Agway store on the left of NY 32. Turn right onto Bear Swamp Road (County Route 404) and cross the Basic Creek Reservoir. Take Bear Swamp Road approximately 1.75 miles past this reservoir to the preserve parking lot and entrance sign on your left (south). (Eastern New York Chapter)

20 *Limestone Rise*

KNOX, ALBANY COUNTY
62 ACRES

 Walk into the Limestone Rise Preserve from Nash Road and you will pass through two distinct natural habitats before you get to this site's signature community. One of these habitats is a glacially formed ridge covered with second-growth woodland, and the other is a small wetland with open water surrounded by brush or swamp willow (*Salix nigra*) and water smartweed (*Polygonum amphibium* var. *emersum*). Neither of these areas, however, prepares you for the diversity of plant life fostered by the lime-rich soils found after the trail crosses to the south side of NY 146.

Here, the frequent rocky outcrops are covered with moss and the ground is thick with herbaceous plants, including sharp-lobed hepatica (*Hepatica nobilis* var. *acuta*), which blooms from April to mid-May, and barren strawberry (*Waldsteinia fragarioides*), which follows until late May. There are frequent crevices along this part of the trail, so you will want to take care and be sure of your footing.

You will see at least a dozen species of fern in this part of the preserve, including walking fern (*Camptosorus rhizophyllus*), which flourishes in lime-rich soil. These ferns derive their name from their peculiar way of dispersing: Miniature ferns, complete

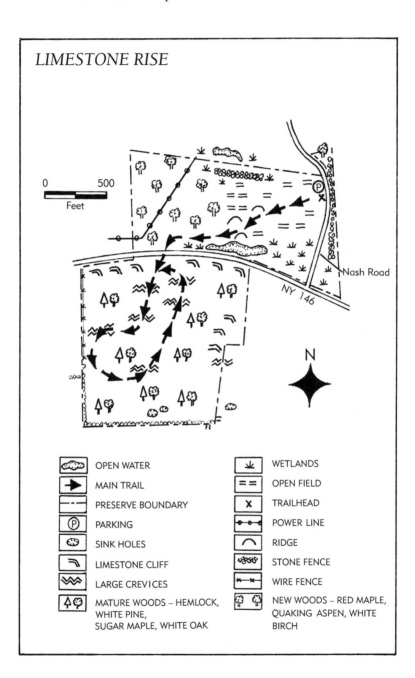

LIMESTONE RISE

0   500
Feet

Nash Road

NY 146

N

OPEN WATER		WETLANDS	
MAIN TRAIL		OPEN FIELD	
PRESERVE BOUNDARY		TRAILHEAD	
PARKING		POWER LINE	
SINK HOLES		RIDGE	
LIMESTONE CLIFF		STONE FENCE	
LARGE CREVICES		WIRE FENCE	
MATURE WOODS – HEMLOCK, WHITE PINE, SUGAR MAPLE, WHITE OAK		NEW WOODS – RED MAPLE, QUAKING ASPEN, WHITE BIRCH	

with root systems, form at the end of the mature fern fronds; as the new growth gets heavier, it bends the "parent" frond to the ground, thereby allowing the offshoot to take root, mimicking a "walking" motion.

The forest here consists mostly of sugar maple (*Acer saccharum*) and eastern hophornbeam (*Ostrya virginiana*), the latter being a small tree with a shaggy, reddish-brown bark, birchlike leaves, and a distinctive cluster of hoplike seed-bearing pods that make the fruit seem packaged in little paper bags. The understory consists of witch-hazel (*Hamamelis virginiana*) and striped maple (*Acer pensylvanicum*); anyone who carved walking sticks at camp as a youngster will remember the latter as "moosewood."

Limestone Rise is part of the Helderburg Escarpment, a range formed when the European and North American continental plates collided. This dramatic geological event also caused the Adirondack and Taconic Mountains to rise. Fossils are richly distributed throughout the limestone, with three kinds especially abundant: *tentaculitis,* an extinct form of marine animal, represented by a small cone-shaped shell with encircling ridged rings (shells are ¼-inch to ½-inch long); *leperditia,* a small crustacean; and *spirifer,* a small brachiopod. The parallel arrangement of tentaculitis shells, mud pebbles, mud and faint ripple marks in the rock all indicate tidal flat conditions at Limestone Rise during the Devonian period, when this rock was formed, some 350 million years ago. These fossils, many of which are similar to those found in rocks on the European continent, provide a crucial link in the geological histories of the continents on either side of the North Atlantic.

Please be careful of the fossils here, and do not disturb them—they are most definitely *not* a renewable resource and should be allowed to remain for future generations to study.

From the entrance on Nash Road follow the trail into the successional old field/successional woods in front of you, keeping the wetland area on your left. Cross NY 146 to the south, where you will see a rather striking limestone ledge. The terrain throughout the southern portion of the preserve is uneven, so be prepared. This trail loops back on itself before rejoining the trail crossing NY 146 to the north on which you entered the preserve. The entire lasso-like loop takes at least 1 hour, at a leisurely pace.

ACQUISITION

This preserve was donated by Earl and Jane Bucci in 1974 and 1979.

DIRECTIONS

From the intersection of US 20 and NY 146 northwest of Albany, take NY 146 west through Altamont. Approximately 4.5 miles past the village of Altamont, you will cross County Route 252 (Knox Cave Road). A few hundred feet past County Route 252 on the right (north) side of the road, you will see Nash Road and a preserve sign on the side of the road. The trail entrance is 0.25 mile up Nash Road on the left side at the top of a small hill. Please do not block the farm entrance across Nash Road, which is marked by a painted metal gate. (Eastern New York Chapter)

21 *Christman Sanctuary*

DUANESBERG, SCHENECTADY COUNTY
95 ACRES

 Formerly part of the Christman Farmstead, which has been designated a registered National Historic Landmark, this land was first purchased and farmed in 1854 by Spencer Christman. His son, the "farmer-poet of the Helderhills," W.W. Christman, stopped farming in 1903 to devote his life to writing poetry. Will Christman won the John Burroughs Memorial Association Award for his collection, "Wild Pasture Pine," which describes much about his life on this land, in a manner that critics of the time likened to Whitman. At 65, Christman established a wildlife sanctuary on the farm, reforesting about 60 acres with black locust (*Robinia pseudo-acacia*), eastern white pine (*Pinus strobus*), red pine (*P. resinosa*), Scotch pine (*P. sylvestris*), and a non-native species of tamarack (*Larix decidua*) also known as European larch. Nature has slowly reclaimed the rest of the farm, determining its present state.

Tamarack is interesting because it is the only northern conifer (cone-bearing tree) that sheds its needles in autumn. The Mohawks and Hudson River Mahicans, who formerly populated this region, used the roots of the native species of tamarack (*Larix lar-*

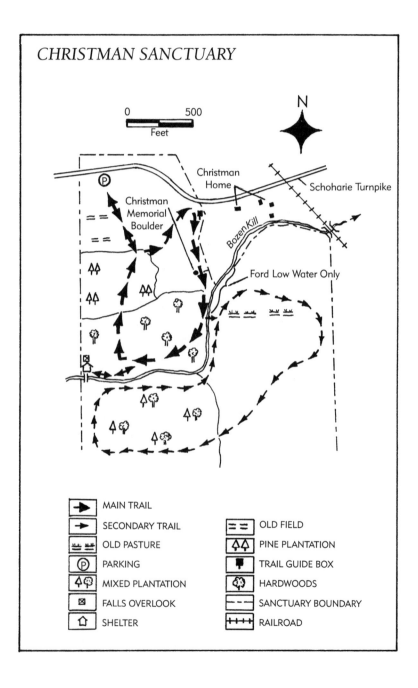

CHRISTMAN SANCTUARY

0 — 500
Feet

N

Christman Home

Schoharie Turnpike

Christman Memorial Boulder

Bozen Kill

Ford Low Water Only

➤	MAIN TRAIL		= =	OLD FIELD
➤	SECONDARY TRAIL		⚗⚗	PINE PLANTATION
⚘	OLD PASTURE		⚑	TRAIL GUIDE BOX
Ⓟ	PARKING		⚘	HARDWOODS
⚘⚘	MIXED PLANTATION		- - -	SANCTUARY BOUNDARY
⊠	FALLS OVERLOOK		┼┼┼┼	RAILROAD
⌂	SHELTER			

icina)—also known as American larch—to sew strips of birch bark together into their ubiquitous canoes. John Josselyn, a Massachusetts Bay Colony naturalist, recalled that the natives also used a turpentine from the tamarack "to heal wounds, and to draw out the malice . . . of any Ache [by] rubbing the place therewith." Happening upon a grove of tamarack in autumn or winter, you would be hard-pressed to believe that a tree with such a lifeless appearance could have restorative powers.

Will Christman came to feel that he was deeply rooted in this land and the surrounding area. Late in life (he died in 1937), as he began to think of the inevitable "planting" of his own body in the soil, he mused on the natural wonders he would leave as his legacy:

> I leave my harvest and good will
> To red poll, siskin and cross-bill:
> To every singing soul good cheer:
> Some walker of the snow may hear
> The ringing carol of the shrike
> Where the first shafts of sunrise strike.
>
> I give, bequeath, devote, devise
> Shelter to every bird that flies;
> Harbor to all that walk or creep;
> To the red fox a bed for sleep;
> Table and roof for every guest
> And place for dove and thrush to nest.
>
> Years hence, some boy driving tranquil,
> Slow cattle up the pasture hill,
> On a spring morning dewy and sweet
> When the field sparrows stay his loitering feet
> Shall see my pine spires tipped with sun
> And hear the thrushes carillon.

The Christman Memorial Boulder proclaims: "His ashes nourish these trees his hands planted."

Christman loved the Bozenkill and wrote extensively about this creek that runs through the sanctuary as it cuts through sandstone and shale. These layers of rock are part of the Schenectady formation, which was formed in a shallow sea in Ordovician times (approximately 450 million years ago). The forest along the Bozenkill is a mature one of sugar maple (*Acer saccharum*), eastern hemlock (*Tsuga canadensis*), American beech (*Fagus grandifolia*), oak (*Quercus* sp.), white ash (*Fraxinus americana*), basswood (*Tilia americana*), and bitternut hickory (*Carya cordiformis*). The understory includes striped maple (*Acer pensylvanicum*), witchhazel (*Hamamelis virginiana*), and ground yew (*Taxus canadensis*).

The trail begins at the parking lot along the Schoharie Turnpike and proceeds through an old apple orchard and pasture to a guide box, which contains a guest book. The trail then follows along a fence dividing the sanctuary from the homestead. Be on the lookout for spring flowers such as Dutchman's breeches (*Dicentra cucullaria*), foamflower (*Tiarella cordifolia*), and trout-lily (*Erythronium americanum*).

A few hundred feet from the Christman Memorial Boulder you may want to take a left onto the Orange (Plantation) Trail that fords the Bozenkill and then loops through the old pasture and into Will Christman's reforestation experiment. (This 2-mile loop is well worth it if you are looking for birds.)

The Blue Trail continues along the hardwood forest lining the Bozenkill. When you come to another fork in the trail, bear left to head down to a shelter next to the falls' plunge pool. Return on the Blue Trail, through the pine plantations to the parking lot. This Blue Trail loop takes about 1 hour.

ACQUISITION

This acreage was purchased from Lansing Christman (Will Christman's son) and family in 1970.

DIRECTIONS

Take US 20 west from Albany to the Schoharie Turnpike, roughly 3 miles east of Duanesburg. Follow this road south approximately 3 miles (where it becomes County Route 2D) to the parking area on the east side of Schoharie Turnpike. (Eastern New York Chapter)

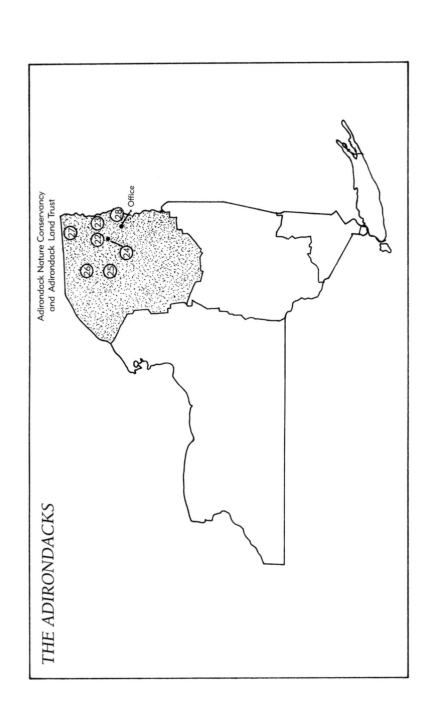

THE ADIRONDACKS

Adirondack Nature Conservancy
and Adirondack Land Trust

Office

The Adirondacks

Comprising 6 million acres, the Adirondacks region is larger than Yellowstone, Yosemite, the Grand Canyon, Glacier, and Olympic National Parks *combined.* With over 2759 lakes and ponds, 32,000 miles of rivers, streams, and brooks, and 46 mountains that are higher than 4000 feet, the Adirondack Mountains are the largest recreation-oriented wildland resource in the eastern United States. Over 130,000 people live here year-round and the region is a popular destination for the more than 70 million people who live within a day's drive of its splendor.

In addition, the Adirondacks region boasts the largest old-growth forest east of the Mississippi, 82 types of natural community (of which 12 are rated among the best examples in the world), 247 rare species, *and* the source of the Hudson River. This *is* a Last Great Place—a vast refuge with large, intact landscapes that give nature the "elbow room" it needs to survive and thrive.

The Adirondack Nature Conservancy/Adirondack Land Trust (ANC/ALT) partnership recognizes the global significance of the Adirondacks and the need for creative and vigilant protection. ANC/ALT's conservation plan for the Adirondacks identifies an interconnected system of nine extremely important core areas that represent the complete array of biodiversity within the region, surrounded by buffer areas—land used for a variety of human activities that are compatible with biodiversity conservation goals. The Conservancy's vision is to protect these core areas and link them across the landscape in ways that allow human activity and biological processes to flourish side by side.

Most importantly, the ANC/ALT wants to safeguard against the loss of any aspect of this rich natural heritage.

22 *Silver Lake Preserve*

BLACK BROOK, CLINTON COUNTY
60.8 ACRES

 The pine bluffs at Silver Lake Preserve offer a panoramic view with a "classic" Adirondack feeling. The lake itself rests between the peaks of the Whiteface and Silver Lake Mountains. In addition, this preserve contains several distinct plant communities, including representative examples of a northern white cedar swamp and a black spruce–tamarack bog. Formerly a portion of the Silver Lake Girl's Camp, the area is often used by school groups for research and education.

The forested wetland that comprises a large portion of the preserve is home to barred owls (*Strix varia*), two species of thrushes, Nashville and yellow-rumped warblers (*Vermivora ruficapilla* and *Dendroica coronata*), and solitary vireos (*Vireo solitarius*). Shorttail shrews (*Blarina brevicauda*) also call this preserve home, daily consuming at least their own weight, generally between ⅖ and ⅘ of an ounce, from the insects on the forest floor.

On the upland portions of the preserve, American beech (*Fagus grandifolia*), yellow birch (*Betula alleghanensis*), and maple (*Acer* sp.) take over, providing feeding grounds for the thrush known as veery (*Hylocichla fuscescens*), black-and-white warblers

SILVER LAKE PRESERVE

Silver Lake Rd.

Union Falls Rd.

Silver Lake

N

0   100
Feet

PRESERVE BOUNDARY

MAIN TRAIL

BOARDWALK

PARKING

BLUFFS

PRESERVE SIGN

HEMLOCK, BALSAM FIR, RED SPRUCE

BEECH, MAPLE, BIRCH

SPRUCE, NORTHERN WHITE, CEDAR, BLACK SPRUCE, SWAMP

(*Mniotilta varia*), warbling vireos (*Vireo gilvus*), wood thrushes (*Hylocichla mustelina*), and eastern wood pewees (*Contopus virens*).

Fishers (*Martes pennanti*) feed on porcupines (*Erethizon dorsatum*), expertly turning them over on their backs and attacking their soft underbellies. Black bears (*Ursus americanus*) flourish atop the pine bluffs. Red squirrels (*Tamiasciurus hudsonicus*) are a particularly vociferous addition to the fauna found at Silver Lake Camp, but they often fall prey to the broad-winged hawks (*Buteo platypterus platypterus*) who nest in the pine canopy.

The boardwalk can be slippery when wet. The rest of the trail is often wet year-round and is recommended only for sturdy hikers with waterproof boots. *Note: Early May through June is blackfly* (Simulium *sp.*) *season, so be sure to bring along insect repellent when visiting the preserve during this time of year.*

From the boardwalk, you can utilize the useful interpretive guide found in the guide box to note such representative bog plants as leatherleaf (*Chamaedaphne calyculata*) and northern pitcher plant (*Sarracenia purpurea*). The latter is an insectivorous plant with tubular leaves that invite unsuspecting insects to enter. Once inside, the bugs are prevented from escaping by stiff hairs that point down the throatlike opening of its leaves. Victims of this plant will eventually fall to the base of the leaf (presumably exhausted by attempting to get out) and are decomposed and digested by the hungry plant.

You should also note the dense "lawn" of sphagnum moss (*Sphagnum* sp.) on either side of the boardwalk; the moss consists of small green living cells surrounded by large, buoyant, water-filled cells that keep the plants afloat. Locally there are about 15 distinct species or taxa of this highly adapted plant, each extracting minerals from the water on which it rests.

As you continue along the boardwalk, notice the diversity of trees and ferns that inhabit Silver Lake Preserve. Trees include yellow birch (*Betula alleghanensis*) and paper birch (*B. papyrifera*),

Pausing along the boardwalk at Silver Lake Preserve

black ash (*Fraxinus nigra*), red spruce (*Picea rubens*) and black spruce (*P. mariana*), northern white cedar (*Thuja occidentalis*), eastern hemlock (*Tsuga canadensis*), and tamarack (*Larix laricina*)—this last is the only non–evergreen conifer in the northeast. Of the ferns, the most prominent is cinnamon fern (*Osmunda cinnamomea*), but crested shield (*Dryopteris cristata*), marsh fern (*Thelypteris palustris*), and mountain woodfern (*Dryopteris campyloptera*) are also present.

Understory plants at Silver Lake Preserve include mountain holly (*Nemopanthus mucronatus*), sheep laurel (*Kalmia angustifolia*), black huckleberry (*Gaylussica baccata*), and Labrador tea (*Ledum groenlandicum*). Leatherleaf is a prominent low shrub in this community and its presence is very important to other bog plants—its branches provide a framework for the root systems of many other species.

From the end of the boardwalk you may wish to continue along the Pine Bluff Trail. This trail winds through a northern hardwood forest and eventually to the bluffs, from which you can gain the "classic Adirondack feeling" referred to above. Retrace your steps along the trail, returning to the boardwalk and back to the parking area.

The boardwalk takes at least 50 minutes; the Pine Bluff Trail will add another 50–60 minutes to your trip, depending upon how much time you spend enjoying the bluffs.

ACQUISITION

Silver Lake Preserve was a gift of Betty Hicks, Hazel Kinzly, and Gladys Larson Pasel in 1975 and 1976.

DIRECTIONS

Take exit 34 near Keeseville off of the Northway (I-87); head west-southwest toward Lake Placid on NY 9N. In the town of Au Sable Forks, take North Main to Silver Lake Road; go 10 miles to Hawkeye (northwest). In Hawkeye, turn left onto Union Falls Road. The preserve is off Union Falls Road on the left—Old Hawkeye Road, which is a dirt road. A sign at the small parking area will direct you to the trail leading to the boardwalk. (Adirondack Nature Conservancy)

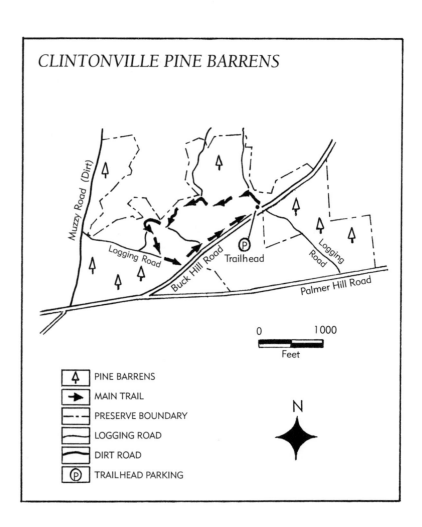

CLINTONVILLE PINE BARRENS

PINE BARRENS
MAIN TRAIL
PRESERVE BOUNDARY
LOGGING ROAD
DIRT ROAD
TRAILHEAD PARKING

N

0   1000
Feet

23 *Clintonville Pine Barrens*

CLINTONVILLE, CLINTON COUNTY
182.84 ACRES

Two New York State–rare plants, prairie redroot (*Ceanothus herbaceus*), known from only two sites in New York, and Houghton's umbrella sedge (*Cyperus houghtonii*), as well as two rare moths, *Xylena thoracica* and *Lithophane lepida lepida*, are what distinguish this pitch pine–heath barrens. Pitch pine–heath barrens are a unique natural community characterized by a fairly open canopy of pitch pine above a concentration of low-growing heath shrubs.

Pitch pine (*Pinus rigida*) can easily be identified by looking at the needles, which form in bundles of three. The foliage is relatively open and the cones may remain on the limbs for several years. Fire is a necessary component of the life-cycle of pitch pine and The Nature Conservancy plans to conduct controlled or prescribed burns as part of the long-term management of these pine barrens. Heat from fire not only opens the cones and releases seeds, but it also releases nutrients from fallen needles and debris, making a seed bed for the eventual regeneration of the barrens.

Pitch pine is the dominant pine of the renowned Pine Barrens of New Jersey, as well as of Cape Cod and Long Island. Its short, rugged trunks are full of knots, which in turn are so full of resin that they were once used as a material for making torches during pioneer days. A bundle of knots tied to a hickory branch will stay lit for hours. In those days, the tar obtained from pitch pine was also used as an axle grease for wagons.

In areas where fires have previously burned, you may see new needles sprouting from buds beneath the bark of the pitch pine. This process, which makes for rather "hairy" looking bark, is called epicormic budding.

Quaking aspen (*Populus tremuloides*) is an invasive species that may also come into an area opened by fire. It is not adapted, however, to frequent fires. These aspens, with their trembling leaves that seem to spin on their stalks, are among the first trees to take hold in burned-over ground. Aspen seedlings can establish new colonies in even the most thoroughly denuded soil, and the trees are remarkably tolerant of sun and drought. When aspens do come up, it is generally in groves of several stems, all rising from the same root. If you look closely at a grove of aspen, it is easy to imagine that you are seeing replicas of only a few trees.

Pitch pine–heath barrens occur in a limited zone between the Canadian jack pine–heath barrens north of the Adirondacks and the pitch pine–scrub oak barrens of New England and Pennsylvania. The Clintonville Pine Barrens occupy a small sandy "bench" between the Ausable and Little Ausable Rivers, and represent an outstanding example of this natural community.

The understory of the pine barrens consists of a number of low-lying shrubs of the heath family, including sheep laurel (*Kalmia angustifolia*) and wintergreen (*Gaultheria procumbens*), as well as blueberry (*Vaccinium* sp.), black huckleberry (*Gaylussacia baccata*), and bearberry (*Arctostaphylos uva-ursi*). In addition, sweet-fern (*Comptonia peregrina*), which has fernlike leaves but woody stems and a flowering reproductive cycle unlike other ferns, is found at Clintonville.

PHOTOGRAPH © THE NATURE CONSERVANCY

Clintonville Pine Barrens

A short, approximately 3500-foot trail follows old logging roads through the preserve. This provides a good overview of the pine barrens ecosystem as it is described above. The trail hooks back to Buck Hill Road, a short distance from where you have parked your car. The entire loop takes about 40 minutes.

ACQUISITION

The Nature Conservancy purchased this land in 1992 and 1993.

DIRECTIONS

From the flashing light in the hamlet of Au Sable Forks on NY 9N, take North Main Street to Golf Course Road, heading northeast approximately 2 miles to the intersection with Palmer Hill Road. (You will see Muzzy Road on the north side of Palmer Hill Road.) Bear right and proceed 0.25 mile to Buck Hill Road on your left. Park at the trailhead off Buck Hill Road about 0.5 mile on the left. (Adirondack Nature Conservancy)

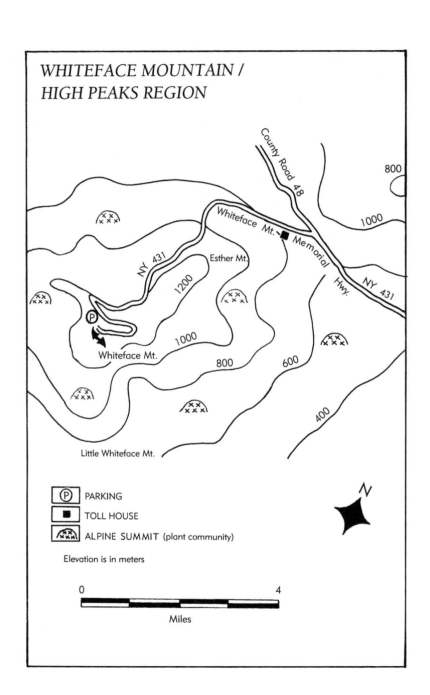

WHITEFACE MOUNTAIN / HIGH PEAKS REGION

County Road 48

800

Whiteface Mt.

1000

NY 431

Esther Mt.

Memorial Hwy.

NY 431

1200

P

1000

Whiteface Mt.

800

600

400

Little Whiteface Mt.

N

P   PARKING

■   TOLL HOUSE

ALPINE SUMMIT (plant community)

Elevation is in meters

0   4

Miles

24 *Whiteface Mountain/High Peaks Region*

SOL GOLDMAN SUMMIT STEWARD PROGRAM
ESSEX COUNTY
85 ACRES
HANDICAPPED ACCESSIBLE

 Although Whiteface Mountain in the High Peaks Region is not a Conservancy preserve, it exemplifies the kind of cooperative program that The Nature Conservancy is involved in throughout the country.

New York State has a little more than 80 acres of arctic alpine meadow habitat and all of it is located in the High Peaks Region of the Adirondacks. The extreme conditions on the mountain summits may seem harsh and forbidding, especially if you happen to be in the High Peaks over the winter, but for the rare, threatened, and endangered plants that make the High Peaks their home, it is paradise.

Paradise, as the poet instructed, is easily lost. It takes thousands of years for enough soil to accumulate on the High Peaks for plants to be able to establish themselves. Although hardy plants such as Lapland rosebay (*Rhododendron lapponicum*) can survive frigid winters and arid summers atop these peaks, erosion caused by wind, water, and insensitive hikers can destroy this mini-habitat in a matter of seconds. The Sol Goldman Summit Steward Program is a joint effort of The Nature Conservancy, the Adirondack Mountain Club, and the New York State Department of Environmental Conservation, designed to educate hikers about the importance of passive, low-impact hiking on the alpine peaks.

The 4867-foot Whiteface Mountain, which is owned by New York State and managed by the Olympic Regional Development Authority, is an easily accessible peak from which to examine these threatened alpine communities. A two-lane toll road, the Whiteface Mountain Veterans Memorial Highway, climbs 3400 feet over an average grade of 8 percent. It terminates merely 276 feet from the summit at Whiteface Castle, where visitors can climb a stone stairway or ride an elevator to the Summit House.

Breathtaking views of Lake Champlain, Vermont's Green Mountains, the St. Lawrence River valley, and the other High Peaks are afforded from atop Whiteface on a clear day. It is a view that Lowell Thomas once referred to as "one of the great scenic vistas of the world." The view is not the only attraction on Whiteface: A short interpretive trail explains the various natural facets of the alpine summit, including the trees, shrubs, herbs, lichens, and mosses that have adapted to the extreme conditions of the area.

DIRECTIONS

From Lake Placid take NY 86 north to Wilmington and the entrance of the Whiteface Mountain Veterans Memorial Highway (NY 431). There is an admission charge for car and driver, with an additional charge per passenger. *Note: Please be careful coming back down the mountain highway; excessive braking can cause a car's brakes to overheat and malfunction.*

25 *Spring Pond Bog*

ALTAMONT, FRANKLIN COUNTY
4289.81 ACRES

Spring Pond Bog is at the heart of the Boreal Heritage Preserve, an
ambitious project created to protect 75,000 acres of prime boreal
wetlands and forests in the Adirondack Park. Much of the
Adirondack Park is part of the Conservancy's initiative "Last
Great Places: An Alliance for People and the Environment." This
is a conservation program designed to protect outstanding ecosystems in the United States, Latin America, and the Pacific. At each
location, the Conservancy is working closely with partners, both
public and private, to demonstrate that economic, recreational,
and other development can occur where nature is being preserved.

The second largest peatland complex in New York State,
Spring Pond Bog includes over 500 acres of open peatland, one of
the largest of these habitats in the northeast. This slightly domed
peatland has raised hummocks or "strings" and valleys or "flarks"
that form a pattern of parallel ridges within the open mat of sedges
and sphagnum moss (*Sphagnum* sp.). Seven to eight hundred acres
of black spruce–tamarack swamp abut this natural community.

Typical northern bog plant species such as northern pitcher

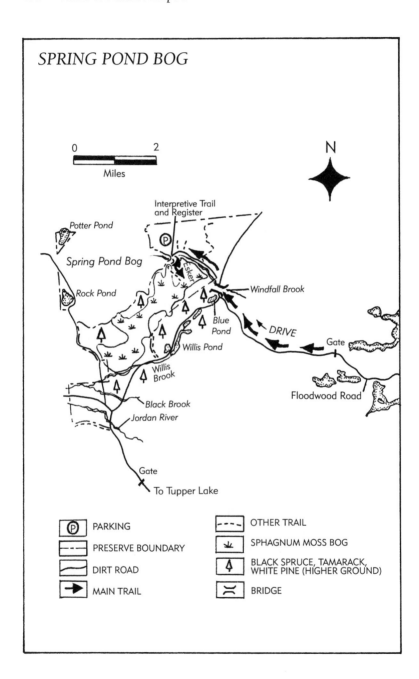

plant (*Sarracenia purpurea*), leatherleaf (*Chamaedaphne calycula-ta*), and Labrador tea (*Ledum groenlandicum*) occur here, as do a number of birds from the New York State–threatened species list: osprey (*Pandion haliaetus carolinensis*), red-shouldered hawk (*Buteo lineatus*), northern harrier or "marsh hawk" (*Circus cyaneus*), and spruce grouse (*Dendragapus canadensis*). This last species nests in ground hollows among the low-hanging conifer branches. Their gregarious and tame nature has earned them the nickname "fool hen."

Contrary to its name, the common raven (*Corvus corax*) is a species of "special concern" in New York, but a number of these large scavengers do live in the bog environs. The gray jay (*Perisoreus canadensis*) is by far the most noticeable character of the Spring Pond Bog, making its presence known by frequent screeching and whistling, and by its call, which sounds like a joyous cowboy's "Whee-ah!" The gray jay has also earned the nickname "Camp Robber" for its practice of raiding food from camps in the north woods. Boreal chickadees (*Parus hudsonicus*), winter wrens (*Troglodytes troglodytes*), red-breasted nuthatches (*Sitta canadensis*), hermit thrushes (*Catharus guttatus*), and two species each of kinglets, flycatchers, and woodpeckers are among the species of birds known to inhabit the bog.

An interpretive trail leads you through this preserve, following along the top of an esker. This esker is the debris resulting from a river that once ran beneath a glacier. A guide is available at the trailhead register. The trail starts within a northern hardwood forest, and you will notice that such typical successionals as sugar maple (*Acer saccharum*), black cherry (*Prunus serotina*), and American beech (*Fagus grandifolia*) dominate this area. Along the esker are a number of sugar maples, as well as red maples (*A. rubrum*) and striped maples (*A. pensylvanicum*) topping off an understory of wintergreen (*Gaultheria procumbens*), blueberry (*Vaccinium* sp.), and bracken fern (*Pteridium aquilinum*).

Spring Pond Bog

PHOTOGRAPH © THE NATURE CONSERVANCY

Further on the trail is a small "teaching bog" containing many of the same plants as the larger Spring Pond Bog. These include examples of few-seeded sedge (*Carex oligosperma*) and white-fringed orchid (*Platanthera blephariglottis*). You may hear the spring song of the olive-sided flycatcher (*Contopus borealis*)— listen for its thirst-provoking call, "quick-three beers, quick-three beers" from the treetops along the bog edge. You can walk down to this bog to examine more closely the sphagnum moss, pitcher plant, and cranberry (*Vaccinium macrocarpon*) of the bog. Footprints can last for decades on the bog mat, however, so please only venture to the edge of this small teaching bog, and not onto Spring Pond Bog itself.

Proceeding along the esker, note a large stand of conifers, including balsam fir (*Abies balsamea*), eastern white pine (*Pinus*

BOG PLANTS GO TO GREAT LENGTHS TO FIND FOOD

Plants and animals that live in peatlands have it tough: High water, low oxygen content, nutrient deficiency, acidity, and an unstable substrate are some of the conditions they have to deal with. Successful peatland species have evolved or adapted strategies to survive under such harsh conditions. One of the most interesting of these adaptations is seen in carnivorous and insectivorous plants.

The northeastern United States has approximately 20 species of carnivorous plants, which can digest insects to obtain nutrients in an otherwise nutrient-poor ecosystem. Most of these carnivorous plants are also able to obtain nutrients through photosynthesis, as other plants do, and typically obtain these extra nutrients during periods of stress.

Carnivorous plants may "catch" their prey either passively or actively. Passive methods include "flypaperlike" pitfalls—the insect enters but cannot climb out of the trap. More active methods have been developed by plants such as the Venus Flytrap (*Dionaea muscipula*) and bladderworts (*Utricularia* spp.), which entrap their victims by snapping shut on the unsuspecting insects.

strobus), and tamarack (*Larix laricina*), along with birds that enjoy this environment: golden-crowned kinglet (*Regulus satrapa*), winter wren, and black-capped chickadee (*Parus atricapillus*). Plants to look for along this trail are bracken fern and twinflower (*Linnaea borealis*).

At the trail's end, you will have a view of the 500-acre, open, mostly treeless bog mat. Spring Pond Bog is an acidic, nutrient-poor peatland that receives most of its water from the atmosphere. As a result of its high acidity, decomposition is slow to occur in the bog, hence its fragility. Animal bodies found in some acidic bogs have been recovered intact some hundred years after they were lost. *Note: The bog itself is extremely fragile; please be careful to stay on the trail. Please do not walk on the bog.* The entire trip can be accomplished in 1 hour.

ACQUISITION
Spring Pond Bog was purchased between 1985 and 1987.

DIRECTIONS
You will need to obtain permission to enter the Spring Pond Bog Preserve. The preserve is located 9 miles north of Tupper Lake. Please call the Adirondack Nature Conservancy office in Keene Valley (see appendix 2) for written permission and directions. (Adirondack Nature Conservancy)

26 *Everton Falls Preserve*

SANTA CLARA, FRANKLIN COUNTY
530 ACRES

 This preserve was once the hamlet of Everton, a 19th-century logging community that was abandoned in the 1890s when the marketable timber was exhausted. Since then, the woods have returned, including balsam fir (*Abies balsamea*), northern white cedar (*Thuja occidentalis*), eastern white pine (*Pinus strobus*), and spruce (*Picea* sp.), along with a number of hardwoods and mature trees that were left standing by the loggers. An interpretive trail through the hardwood forest is an excellent way to learn about the phases of forest succession.

The trailhead of the Hardwoods Trail was once a "skidway," where loggers piled logs to be loaded onto trucks during the last logging operation in these woods (1960s). Mosses and perennials such as goldenrod (*Solidago* sp.) and spiraea (*Spiraea* sp.), as well as shrubs and young trees prosper in this disturbed area, along with pink earth lichen (*Baeomyces roseus*) (notice the gray crust with pink fruit). Lichen is a combination of fungus and alga that have a mutually beneficial relationship, exemplifying a "good neighbor policy": the alga provides food for the fungus, and in return is protected from drought by its cohabitant.

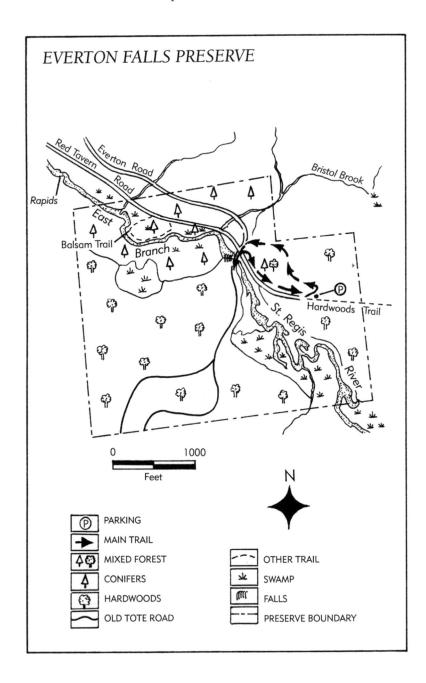

EVERTON FALLS PRESERVE

The trail leads first to a beaver pond—the product of a beaver colony that returned more than 10 years ago. On the north shore is the beaver lodge, and you can see traces of recent beaver activity in the number of cuttings across the pond. As you pass the beaver pond, notice the proliferation of Canada mayflower (*Maianthemum canadense*) and goldenrod by the side of the trail.

Further along, you should begin to notice a rather prominent shrub known as witch-hobble or hobblebush (*Viburnum lantanoides*). In all likelihood you may be forced to notice it—its drooping low branches often take root at the terminus, forming hooks or loops that can easily trip you up if you are not careful. This species of *Viburnum* is widespread in the Adirondacks. In mid- to late May, its conspicuous blossoms form a broad, pancakelike cluster with an outside ring of its most distinctive flowers. In the fall, its berries perform a dramatic color change, turning from coral to crimson to purple.

The tree clubmoss (*Lycopodium obscurum*) is another highly distinctive plant in these woods. Look for what appear to be miniature evergreens; in fact, tree clubmoss, along with other species of "ground pines," were once in great demand as ornamental elements during the Christmas season.

The spores of many clubmosses were also used to make lycopodium powder for use in flashpowder for photography and as an anti-chafing agent. Clubmosses are so called because of their habit of producing spores on "clubs." One species of clubmoss at this preserve, shining clubmoss (*Huperzia lucidulum*), however, produces its spores in the axils of its leaves. You can easily identify shining clubmoss by keeping in mind one of its historical nicknames: "staghorn moss."

The clearing toward the end of the Hardwoods Trail marks the location of what was formerly Everton. Notice the unpaved extension of Red Tavern Road; long ago it was a section of the Port Kent–Hopkinton Turnpike, the most important stop on the log-

PHOTOGRAPH © THE NATURE CONSERVANCY

Everton Falls

ging railway from St. Regis Falls. The hamlet sported a sawmill, a tavern, and an inn, around which the community grew.

The meadow now provides fine examples of many summer wildflowers, including Joe-Pye weed (*Eupatorium maculatum*), and fireweed (*Epilobium angustifolium*). Look for rose-breasted grosbeaks (*Pheucticus ludovicianus*) in early May, when they are busy eating larvae, buds, and seeds from the trees.

When you come to the end of the trail, cross Red Tavern Road to the bank of the East Branch of the St. Regis River and a brief, unmarked trail to the falls for which this preserve was named. Upstream from the falls, the East Branch has a trout stream and an open 10-mile stretch of canoeable stillwater that marks a basin once filled by a postglacial lake. The entire trip takes 1 hour, depending upon time spent at the falls.

ACQUISITION

This land was purchased from Mr. Harry McManus in 1974.

DIRECTIONS

From NY 3 between Tupper Lake and Saranac Lake take NY 30 north toward the town of Malone. At Duane Center look for signs for NY 99 (on your right), at which you will take a left onto County Route 14 (Red Tavern Road), an extension of NY 99. Traveling west on Red Tavern Road approximately 7 miles, you will come to the entrance of the Hardwoods Trail on your right shortly after passing the Red Tavern itself. (Adirondack Nature Conservancy)

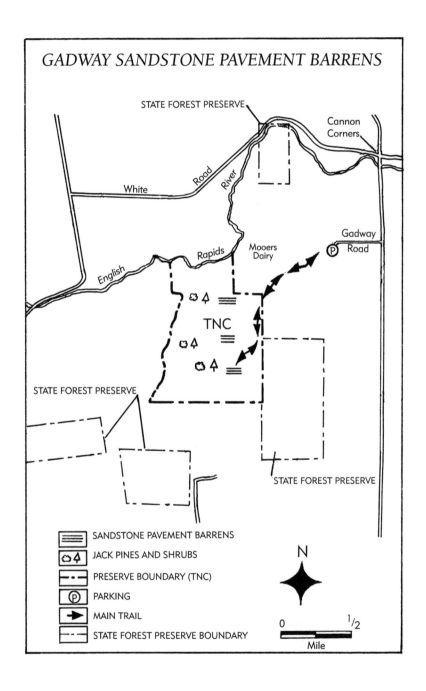

GADWAY SANDSTONE PAVEMENT BARRENS

STATE FOREST PRESERVE

Cannon Corners

White

Road

River

English

Rapids

Mooers Dairy

Gadway
Road

TNC

STATE FOREST PRESERVE

STATE FOREST PRESERVE

SANDSTONE PAVEMENT BARRENS

JACK PINES AND SHRUBS

PRESERVE BOUNDARY (TNC)

PARKING

MAIN TRAIL

STATE FOREST PRESERVE BOUNDARY

N

0   1/2
Mile

27 Gadway Sandstone Pavement Barrens

TOWN OF MOOERS, CLINTON COUNTY
335 ACRES

 Located in a region otherwise dominated by dairy farms and sugar bushes, Gadway Barrens represent an outstanding example of sandstone pavement barrens, a globally rare natural community known from fewer than 20 sites in the world. These were formed during the glacial retreat of the last Ice Age. As the ice sheet melted, a catastrophic flood took with it all of the vegetation from the bedrock. What was left is an outcropping of Potsdam sandstone that in turn originated as quartz beach sand 500 million years ago.

As you venture into this preserve, you will notice what appears to be a series of paved roads resembling a vast network of avenues that would make Caesar envious. The impression is of having stumbled upon the ruins of an ancient palatial garden, as the scrubby jack pine (*Pinus banksiana*), chokeberry (*Aronia melanocarpa*), blueberry (*Vaccinium* sp.), and black huckleberry (*Gaylussacia baccata*) bushes of the barrens almost appear to be "planted" in groves between the exposed sandstone pavement. The only thing missing is the old sandstone palace itself.

What you are actually seeing is the exposed level bedrock, which is often covered only by lichens and mosses, including reindeer lichen (*Cladina* sp.), *Cladonia* sp., haircap lichen (*Polytrichum* sp.), and common redstem (*Pleurozium schreberi*). Bracken fern (*Pteridium aquilinum*) grows in the mossy carpet, along with wintergreen (*Gaultheria procumbens*) and poverty grass (*Danthonia spicata*).

Jack pines, considered rare in New York State, are one of the few trees that can endure the dry, nutrient-poor soils of the barrens. Over the last 10,000 years, these trees and shrubs have been able to colonize the thin soil, but the process is slow. The harsh conditions of this environment have caused the 80- to 100-year-old trees to take on such twisted and gnarled forms that you can touch the treetops with a modicum of effort.

Jack pines have a very curious anecdotal history, especially in the provinces of Canada to the north of Gadway. Canadian lumberjacks believed that jack pines could turn sterile any woman who passed by them—apparently closing their wombs like the closed cones of the pines, which can remain unopened on the trees for years without releasing their seeds. These jack pine cones are curiously humpbacked, curving out from their base to form a delicate point. They can, in fact, stay on the tree almost indefinitely before finally dropping their seeds to the wind. Judging by the number of children to be seen in Mooers and nearby towns, the suggestion that jack pines cause sterility would seem to be greatly exaggerated.

The jack pine barrens are populated by fishers (*Martes pennanti*), bobcats (*Lynx rufus*), and white-tailed deer (*Odocoileus virginianus*), all of which vacate the premises during the hottest and driest summer weather. These animals are smart enough to know when to head off to more densely forested lands. The same is true for the deer mice (*Peromyscus maniculatus*) and boreal redback voles (*Clethrionomys gapperi*), who burrow deep underground

PHOTOGRAPH © THE NATURE CONSERVANCY

Gadway Sandstone Pavement Barrens

during drought or heat wave; you can sometimes see them scurrying about the sandstone or, in the case of the voles, climbing into the jack pines to eat.

After parking your car, walk along Gadway Road, the only trail into the preserve. There is no loop here, so the length of your trip is entirely up to you; after parking your car, walk a little way into the preserve and then retrace your steps back to your car. Much of the early part of this trail crosses private property, so please respect the easement the Conservancy has been granted to access the preserve. A compass is recommended, as much of the terrain is similar and it is easy to become disoriented.

ACQUISITION

An initial gift of 285 acres from the Patton Corporation was accepted in 1989; additional purchase of 50 acres was made in 1990.

DIRECTIONS

From NY 30 in the town of Malone, take US 11 east toward Mooers and Rouses Point. A few miles out of Ellenburg, look for Cannon Corners Road on your left. Follow Cannon Corners Road approximately 1.5 miles north of US 11. Gadway Road can be a little difficult to find (it is unmarked and looks like a private driveway), but it is on the left almost directly opposite a large grove of maples and next to Mooers Dairy.

Follow Gadway Road approximately 0.5 mile through the dairy property, where there is a small clearing for parking cars. The dirt and sandstone road runs through privately owned land that extends into the preserve. The Conservancy has an easement on the road for access to the preserve. (Adirondack Nature Conservancy)

28 *Coon Mountain Preserve*

WADHAMS, ESSEX COUNTY
168 ACRES

 Coon Mountain is part of the Adirondack Land Trust's Champlain Valley Farm and Forest Project. The mountain itself includes many steep rock faces, small wetlands, streams, and a mixed hardwood forest. An unmarked trail to the craggy summit affords views of Lake Champlain, the Green Mountains of Vermont, and the Adirondack High Peaks.

The Champlain Valley Farm and Forest Project was designed to protect the various components of the area's working landscape: farms, sustainable forestry, natural and scenic areas, and open space recreational resources. The Coon Mountain Preserve is an example of the Adirondack Nature Conservancy and Adirondack Land Trust's commitment to the local community. A 73-acre site adjacent to the preserve is protected by a Land Trust conservation easement allowing sustainable forestry practices that help support a local mill. To the northwest of the preserve is Little Falls Farm, a working farm also protected by a Land Trust easement.

Coon Mountain itself was logged for charcoal to fuel nearby Merriam's Forge during the Civil War. Five small rocky summits are surrounded by a dry, open, red oak–white pine forest that holds

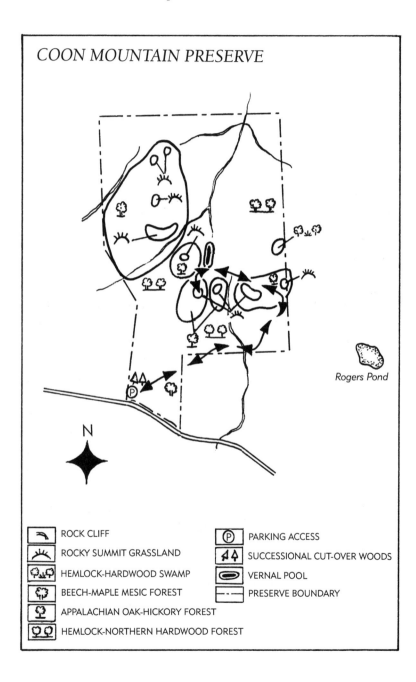

COON MOUNTAIN PRESERVE

Rogers Pond

N

ROCK CLIFF		PARKING ACCESS	
ROCKY SUMMIT GRASSLAND		SUCCESSIONAL CUT-OVER WOODS	
HEMLOCK-HARDWOOD SWAMP		VERNAL POOL	
BEECH-MAPLE MESIC FOREST		PRESERVE BOUNDARY	
APPALACHIAN OAK-HICKORY FOREST			
HEMLOCK-NORTHERN HARDWOOD FOREST			

within it several vernal pools. Vernal pools are shallow depressions that are flooded in spring or after a heavy rainfall, but are generally dry during summer months. Because these pools are temporary, they are unable to support fish who feed on the eggs of amphibians. Thus, wood frogs (*Rana sylvatica*), red-spotted newts (*Notophthalmus viridescens viridescens*), and mole salamanders (*Ambystoma* spp.) depend on these pools as breeding areas. Hawks use the rocky outcrops, and the hemlock–northern hardwood and beech–maple forests of Coon Mountain provide habitat for a variety of flora and fauna.

Follow the old logging road along the lower portion of the preserve, until you have just about reached the preserve's eastern boundary. Then, working your way up across some fairly steep terrain, follow the unmarked trail to the summit plateau. (A trail will be built in 1995. Contact the Adirondack Nature Conservancy [see appendix 2] regarding status before your visit.) Remember to bring a topographical map and a good compass. *Note: Please observe the rights of all landowners and hike only on the preserve lands.*

Once atop the summit, head in a northwesterly direction for a pace, then due west for a short stretch, where the terrain dips before ascending to the top of a small ridge. Proceed south along this ridge and you will soon reach the top of a rocky outcrop, from which you will obtain a 240-degree panorama with views of the High Peaks, Lake Champlain, and the Green Mountains. Retrace your steps back to the logging road; this is important because what might appear to be shortcuts can quickly become steep terrain that is difficult to traverse. Turn right at the logging road and follow it back to the parking area.

The entire trip takes a little more than 1 hour. *This hike is recommended for experienced hikers only.*

ACQUISITION

Coon Mountain Preserve was acquired through a land swap in 1991.

DIRECTIONS

From the Northway (I-87) take exit 31 to NY 9N east into West-port, then take NY 22 north to the town of Wadhams. Proceed north about 1 mile, then take a right onto Morrison Road. Cross the Boquet River to the junction with Halds Road. Follow Halds Road to the preserve entrance on the north side, about 1 mile from the junction. Park off the road at an old timber landing. (Adirondack Nature Conservancy)

BATS ADAPT, ADOPTING NEW HIBERNATION HABITAT

There are 20 bat hibernacula (winter shelters) currently documented in the Adirondacks. Three hibernacula, which are found in abandoned mines, are especially significant because they are wintering homes for the federally endangered Indiana bat (*Myotis sodalis*) and large numbers of other bat species. In fact, one of the mines has a winter population of 120,000 bats, making it the largest known bat hibernacula in the northeast.

In this case, man's alteration of the landscape has resulted in a new habitat. Bats may have moved into these northern mines to escape the disturbances created by spelunkers in southern caves or as a result of the decline or loss of roosting habitat.

Finding the right place to winter is not simple. Each bat species requires a specific temperature and humidity range for hibernation. Most caves do not meet these requirements, but the old mines of the Adirondacks do.

Adirondack bats hibernate over the winter when insect food is unavailable, storing as body fat all the fuel necessary to endure the long period of suspended animation. A bat awakened too often during hibernation will die of starvation, while a bat that survives hibernation emerges in the spring, lean and hungry for insects: each can consume a third of its body weight (typically ¼ to ⅓ pound) in insects during a single night.

Adirondack Nature Conservancy/Adirondack Land Trust is protecting the three key bat hibernacula in partnership with International Paper Company, keeping the bats from being disturbed during hibernation and ensuring that the mines remain open and available to them.

CENTRAL AND WESTERN NEW YORK

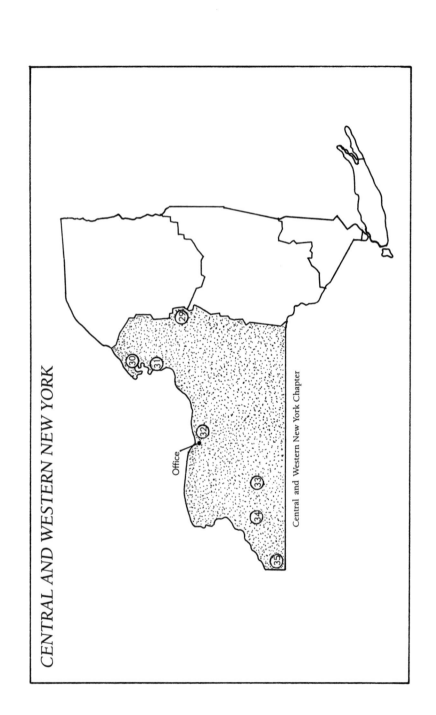

Office

Central and Western New York Chapter

Central and Western New York

Even after 200 years of intense development and cultivation, the central and western region of New York retains astonishing natural diversity. From the limestone barrens of Jefferson County to the hardwood forests of the southern tier, this region boasts 48 distinct types of natural habitats. Some of these barrens, dunes, fens, and swamps are found in few other places on earth. These biological riches contribute incalculably to the quality of life in the region.

Since 1957 the volunteers and professional staff of The Nature Conservancy in central and western New York have taken direct action to protect this region's natural diversity. The chapter owns 26 preserves, over 13,000 acres of biologically significant lands and wetlands, including its first preserve, which protects Moss Lake's beautiful and rich glacial kettlehole bog in Allegheny County, and its most recently established nature sanctuary, which protects the alvar grassland of Chaumont Barrens, a habitat found in fewer than 20 places on earth.

Recently the Conservancy has embarked on a profound but consistent expansion of its work in this region, recognizing that natural communities—like Great Lakes dunes and prairies—are merely parts of the much larger landscapes that surround them. The balance of life inside a nature preserve always depends on ecological processes that extend beyond the protected area—the flow of water, for instance, that keeps a rare fen community alive. And so the Conservancy seeks to protect both natural communities and the natural processes that sustain them.

For example, to protect the mosaic of rare habitats found at Chaumont Barrens, the Conservancy is conducting research on the hydrology of the barrens. An understanding of the role that flooding may play in maintaining unusual prairie habitats will be a key element in the long-term strategy for preserving the barrens.

At French Creek in Chautauqua County, one of the most biologically diverse aquatic systems in the northeast, the chapter is working with public and private partners to protect the flora and fauna of the creek and its watershed, which is home to 66 species of fish and 25 species of mussels. Using a combination of traditional land protection techniques, partnerships with farmers, and research on the survival needs of rare aquatic species, the Conservancy is working to preserve this riverine community.

In this project and in others, the Conservancy seeks to address a fundamental challenge: how to preserve the natural essence of the central and western New York region—and the state—while the landscape supports a growing economy. The Conservancy's approach is to pursue science-based, carefully focused land protection, in cooperation with a network of partners. It is hoped that projects like these will protect natural diversity locally, and also serve as models for new approaches to conservation.

29 Lake Julia Preserve

REMSEN, ONEIDA COUNTY
836.22 ACRES

 Nestled in the foothills of the Adirondacks, Lake Julia Preserve has been called the most diverse and "wild" preserve belonging to The Nature Conservancy in central New York. This is due in part to the fact that it comprises 10 distinct habitats, including an upland deciduous forest, two hemlock–northern hardwood forests, a spruce thicket, a couple of pine plantations, and four brooks. The hardwood forest, which has not been logged since before 1920 and is now approaching its climax stage, consists of sugar maple (*Acer saccharum*) interspersed with red maple (*A. rubrum*), American beech (*Fagus grandifolia*), black cherry (*Prunus serotina*), white or paper birch (*Betula papyrifera*), yellow birch (*B. alleghanensis*), quaking aspen (*Populus tremuloides*), and eastern hemlock (*Tsuga canadensis*). The "primeval" forests of this preserve provide habitat for mink (*Mustela vison*), porcupine (*Erethizon dorsatum*), snowshoe hare (*Lepus americanus*), coyote (*Canis latrans*), white-tailed deer (*Odocoileus virginianus*), and black bear (*Ursus americanus*).

Near the northern border of the preserve, one of the lowland forests merges onto a white spruce thicket and two wooded

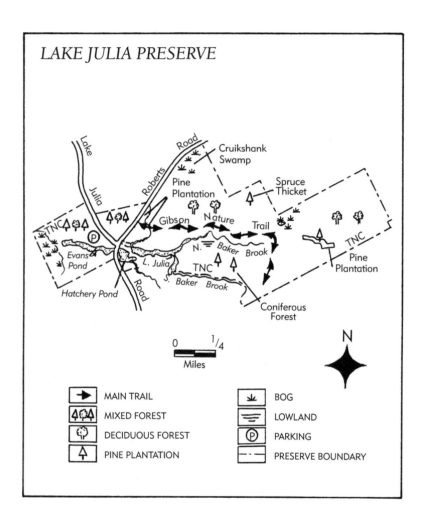

LAKE JULIA PRESERVE

Lake
Julia

Roberts Road

Cruikshank
Swamp

Pine
Plantation

Spruce
Thicket

TNC

Evans
Pond

P

Gibson   Nature   Trail

L. Julia

N. Baker Brook

TNC

TNC

Pine
Plantation

Hatchery Pond

Road

S. Baker Brook

Coniferous
Forest

0   1/4
Miles

N

➤ MAIN TRAIL

🌲🍁🌲 MIXED FOREST

🌳 DECIDUOUS FOREST

🌲 PINE PLANTATION

🌿 BOG

≡ LOWLAND

Ⓟ PARKING

‒ · ‒ PRESERVE BOUNDARY

swamps. One swamp forms a perimeter around a bog and the quaking sphagnum mat that surrounds the bog. Bog plants such as leatherleaf (*Chamaedaphne calyculata*), northern pitcher plant (*Sarracenia purpurea*), round-leaved sundew (*Drosera rotundifolia*), cotton grass (*Eriophorum virginicum*), bog laurel (*Kalmia polifolia*), bog rosemary (*Andromeda polifolia* var. *glaucophylla*), and American cranberry (*Vaccinium macrocarpon*) are present.

Lake Julia was formed by the historic damming of Baker Brook at successive points downstream (as were neighboring Hatchery and Evans Ponds). The Gibson Nature Trail parallels Lake Julia and winds pleasantly through one of the pine plantations planted here by the US government during World War I, and then into the deciduous forest. The trail is approximately 1.5 miles long and there is no loop; you must return the way you came. The walk to the terminus of the Gibson Nature Trail and back takes a little over 1 hour.

ACQUISITION

This land was donated by Cynthia Anne Gibson in 1976 and 1981.

DIRECTIONS

From the New York State Thruway (I-90) take exit 31 at Utica; drive north 15.5 miles on NY 12 to Pritchard Road (County Route 53, at Mondi's BBQ). Turn right onto Pritchard and follow it to the stop sign at Main Street (there will be railroad tracks directly in front of you, across Main). Take a left here and drive 1.1 miles and turn right on Kuyahoora Lake Road (also known as Fairchild Road/County Route 55). Proceed 3.3 miles to Lake Julia Road on the left. There is a small, white chapel (the "Capel Enilli," a Welsh Calvinist Methodist chapel) on the right and the tiny "Enilli Cemetery" on the left. Turn left and proceed 1.2 miles on Lake Julia Road; watch for Evans Pond on your left and Hatchery Pond on your right. Proceed past the ponds and Roberts Road (dirt road on right) approximately 0.25 mile along Lake Julia Road to a parking area on the left. Walk back to Roberts Road. The Gibson Nature Trail begins about 0.25 mile along Roberts Road, on the right, at the base of a small hill. (Central and Western New York Chapter)

30 Chaumont Barrens

LYME AND CLAYTON, JEFFERSON COUNTY
1620 ACRES

 Walking into the Chaumont Barrens is like stepping onto another planet, or at least some part of the midwest where grasslands are more common. Formed by the retreating glaciers over 10,000 years ago, the large areas of limestone bedrock in Jefferson County were washed clean by the retreating glaciers over 10,000 years ago. What was left behind was a natural "pavement" that has since been covered over with thin soils. In some places the soils are so thin that local inhabitants gave the areas names like "Burnt Rock." Indeed, if you come here in high summer, you may think the barrens have been burned: The intense summer sun heats the underlying limestone to such an extreme that the grasses above turn brown and crisp, becoming extremely susceptible to fire.

Almost everyone can remember what it is like to step onto concrete pavement on a summer's day, so it is easy to imagine what these grasses experience each year. Still, they are a hardy bunch, as tough and resilient as the people who live this far north.

Along with calcareous pavement barrens and limestone woodlands, alvar grasslands complete the mosaic of natural communities at this preserve. Alvar grasslands occur in fewer than 20 places

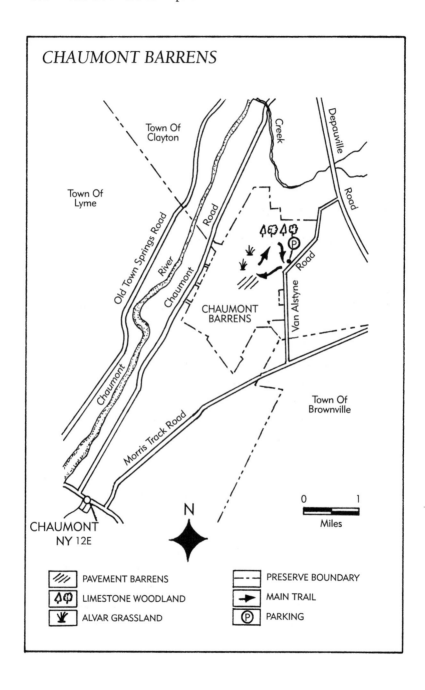

CHAUMONT BARRENS

Town Of Clayton

Town Of Lyme

Town Of Brownville

Creek

Depauville Road

Old Town Springs Road

Chaumont River Road

Chaumont River

Chaumont

CHAUMONT BARRENS

Van Alstyne Road

Morris Track Road

CHAUMONT NY 12E

N

0   1
Miles

PAVEMENT BARRENS

LIMESTONE WOODLAND

ALVAR GRASSLAND

PRESERVE BOUNDARY

MAIN TRAIL

PARKING

in the world, and are characterized by a number of grasses, including tufted hairgrass (*Deschampsia cespitosa*) and prairie dropseed (*Sporobolus heterolepis*), along with sedges like Crawe's (*Carex crawei*), troublesome (*C. molesta*), and chestnut (*C. castanea*). You may also happen upon Indian-paintbrush (*Castilleja coccinea*), along with the New York State–rare prairie smoke (*Geum triflorum*). Until 1984, when New York Natural Heritage Program ecologist Carol Reschke discovered the plant at Chaumont, prairie smoke had not been seen in New York State since botanist John Torrey recorded a sighting in 1842. In fact, before Ms. Reschke's discovery it was thought to have completely disappeared from New York. Many flowering plants have small flowers that are not showy. Prairie smoke, however, has pretty red nodding flowers, which are small but not unremarkable. What makes this flower distinctive from others is its showy, fruiting stem. The stem of the prairie smoke can stretch up to 15 inches tall, so that the three nodding seedheads can be held upright and the seeds may scatter in the wind.

Natural grasslands are an unusual occurrence in the northeast, where woodlands are the dominant natural community. Trees tend to take over most grasslands if the land is left undisturbed. Common natural disturbances, like fire and flood, are needed to keep trees and shrubs from rooting. In alvar grasslands, periodic flooding in the spring followed by summer drought is the regime that helps maintain the grasslands.

The Nature Conservancy is currently planning to restore certain areas of Chaumont Barrens by removing invasive exotic species, such as common buckthorn (*Rhamnus cathartica*). The plan for long-term management of the preserve will ensure the health of the grasslands and its natural systems.

The numerous rocky outcrops that you will see when walking in Chaumont Barrens are surrounded by mosses such as the oddly named outboard motor moss (*Tortella tortuosa*) and worm moss

(*Bryum cespiticium*), along with southern hairgrass (*Agrostis hiemalis*), false pennyroyal (*Trichostema brachiatum*), harebell (*Campanula rotundifolia*), and rough cinquefoil (*Potentilla norvegica*). Notice that where these rocky outcrops occur there are more trees and shrubs than elsewhere on the preserve. These are predominantly eastern red cedar (*Juniperus virginiana*) and northern white cedar (*Thuja occidentalis*), along with bur oak (*Quercus macrocarpa*), eastern white pine (*Pinus strobus*), shagbark hickory (*Carya ovata*), and white ash (*Fraxinus americana*).

Prairie warblers (*Dendroica discolor*) and upland sandpipers (*Bartramia longicauda*) have been observed at Chaumont Barrens, but little is known about the other animals that may live here. There is an abundance of breeding birds at the barrens, including whip-poor-will (*Aprimulgus vociferous*), black and white warbler (*Mniotilta varia*), Cooper's hawk (*Accipiter cooperii*), and Nashville warbler (*Vermivora ruficapilla*).

A 2-mile interpretive trail, to be opened in June 1995, wanders through the full range of this globally rare alvar grassland landscape. Visitors may use the trail from May through October. Hikers should wear sturdy footgear and be prepared for uneven terrain. The trail offers a number of glimpses into the various com-

---

FERTILE BARRENS

After aerial photos of northwestern New York's limestone pavement barrens revealed an unusual plant formation in the Chaumont Barrens, an NHP Conservancy scientist decided to take a closer look. The scientist's survey in the mid-1980s uncovered a small population of rare prairie smoke (*Geum triflorum*), previously believed to have been extirpated in the state.

The discovery of this reddish purple, starlike grassland flower launched the Central and Western New York Chapter's protection efforts in the barrens. Now, these efforts have protected nearly 1620 acres that provide shelter to 16 additional state-threatened species.

ponents of the natural communities at Chaumont Barrens, including open flat limestone plains, rubbly moss-covered expanses, limestone cracks and fissures, deep cedar glades, shrubby and grassy barrens, and a deciduous limestone woodland with an abundance of spring wildflowers.

ACQUISITION

The Nature Conservancy acquired its initial 745 acres at Chaumont Barrens in 1987. Additional acreage was acquired from 1990 to 1992.

DIRECTIONS

Traveling north on I-81, drive past the Watertown exit for Arsenal Street (US 3). The next exit north of Arsenal is for Coffeen Street (NY 12F). Take this exit, and turn left at the light. Proceed about 2 miles to the crossroads of Paddy Hill (you will pass a green sign with the name Paddy Hill on it). In Paddy Hill, turn right and cross the bridge into the village of Brownville. After the bridge, you will come to a T-intersection. This is NY 12E. Turn left at the stop sign and follow NY 12E to Chaumont. Make the first right in the village of Chaumont, onto Morris Track Road. Proceed about 3 miles, just past a small cemetery on the right, to a left turn on Van Alstyne Road. The preserve parking lot is on the left, after about 1.25 miles. (Central and Western New York Chapter)

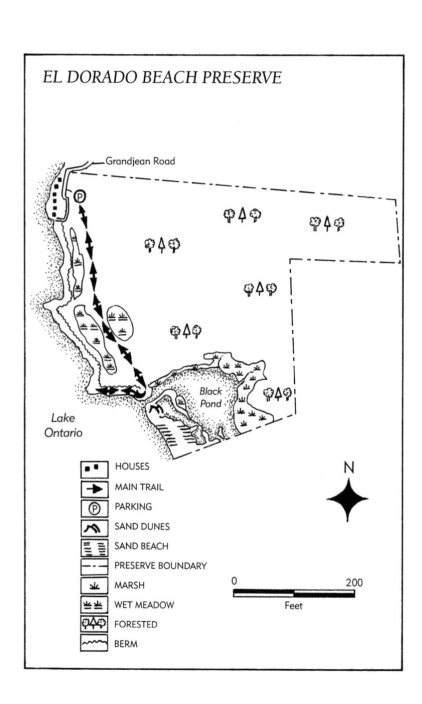

EL DORADO BEACH PRESERVE

Grandjean Road

Black
Pond

Lake
Ontario

■ ▪ HOUSES

→ MAIN TRAIL

Ⓟ PARKING

⌒ SAND DUNES

≣ SAND BEACH

– ‧ – PRESERVE BOUNDARY

⚘ MARSH

⚘⚘ WET MEADOW

🌳🌲🌳 FORESTED

〰 BERM

N

0   200
Feet

31 *El Dorado Beach Preserve*

ELLISBURG, JEFFERSON COUNTY
347.84 ACRES

If you are looking for migrating shorebirds, then El Dorado Beach is for you. Located in the center of a major flyway between James Bay in Ontario and the Atlantic seaboard, El Dorado is frequented by gulls, terns, ducks, herons, and over 25 other species of shorebirds from July through September. What attracts these migrants to this "fueling station" is the abundance of invertebrates that lodge in the algae, *Cladophora,* which accumulates on the shelving sheetrock of the shoreline, a calcareous shoreline outcrop.

The trail begins at the parking area and enters a dense thicket of eastern red cedar (*Juniperus virginiana*) that makes comfortable habitat for concentrations of flycatchers, warblers, vireos, and sparrows from early August through early October. This thicket and the adjacent fields compose the largest area of the preserve. The cedar was logged extensively in the past, mostly for fenceposts. Twenty-five years ago this practice ceased, and in the ensuing time, cedar has steadily increased its presence throughout the preserve.

Continuing south, the trail enters a wet meadow with several

El Dorado Beach Preserve

standing pools, where you may notice blue-winged teals (*Anas dis-cors*) nesting. You will eventually reach the high sand dunes near Black Pond. These Great Lakes dune communities represent some of the least-disturbed high dunes on Lake Ontario. From here proceed north along the trail just upshore from the beach. Shorebirds can be observed from vantage points along the trail without posing undue disturbance to their feeding and nesting.

Depending upon the water level, you may see some large boulders offshore—these are the favorite haunt of double-crested cormorants (*Phalacrocorax auritus*). Above the water's edge the beach becomes what is known as a typical Lake Ontario cobble shore, consisting of water-polished stones of varying sizes and shapes.

Of the many visiting shorebirds, the first to appear are the lesser yellowlegs (*Tringa flavipes*) and least sandpipers (*Calidris minutilla*), who usually arrive around the 4th of July. By midmonth, semipalmated sandpipers (*Calidris pusilla*), short-billed dowitchers (*Limnodromus griseus*), and semipalmated plovers (*Charadrius semipalmatus*) have joined the earlier migrants. After the peak appearances of immature shorebirds around mid- to late August through mid-September, the decline in numbers and variety is fairly rapid. Arguably the best time to visit El Dorado Beach is late July through late August, when the largest numbers of adults of many species can be spotted.

A marked trail from the parking area passes through the cedar glades before reaching the shoreline. Both sandy and rocky shorelines are visible from this trail. From the shore, follow the trail markers for about 100 feet, then retrace your steps back to the parking area. *Note: Please try to stay away from any shorebirds, especially during the peak season (July–September); keeping your distance will disturb the birds as little as possible.* This walk takes approximately 50 minutes.

ACQUISITION

The initial purchase of 252.94 acres was made in 1969; the remainder was purchased in 1982.

DIRECTIONS

Take I-81 north from Syracuse to exit 40, then NY 193/County Route 193 west to NY 3. Turn right (north) onto NY 3 and drive 4 miles. Turn left (west) on Stony Creek Road and watch for the first chance to turn left again, 1.5 miles after leaving NY 3. Follow this road (Grandjean Road) about 0.7 mile. After the last cottage on the left, take the left fork at the "El Dorado Beach Preserve" sign. (Central and Western New York Chapter)

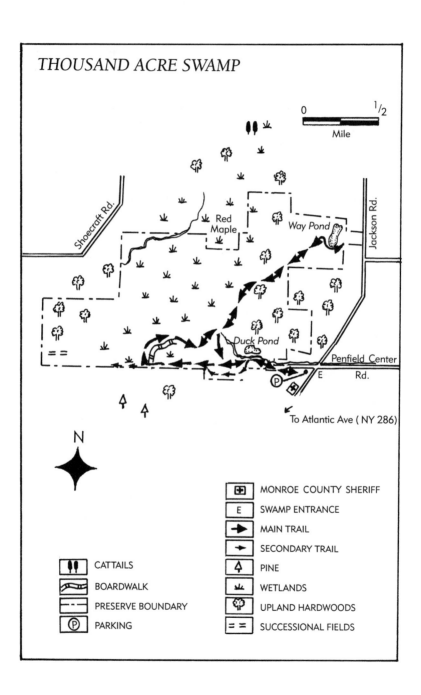

THOUSAND ACRE SWAMP

0 ___ 1/2
Mile

Shoecraft Rd.

Red Maple

Way Pond

Jackson Rd.

Duck Pond

Penfield Center Rd.

P   E

To Atlantic Ave (NY 286)

N

⊞ MONROE COUNTY SHERIFF
E SWAMP ENTRANCE
➤ MAIN TRAIL
→ SECONDARY TRAIL
⌁ PINE
⫰ WETLANDS
🌳 UPLAND HARDWOODS
= = SUCCESSIONAL FIELDS

CATTAILS
BOARDWALK
PRESERVE BOUNDARY
P PARKING

32 *Thousand Acre Swamp*

PENFIELD, MONROE COUNTY
348.98 ACRES
HANDICAPPED ACCESSIBLE

 The Thousand Acre Swamp actually totals around 650 acres, nearly 349 of which are part of The Nature Conservancy's preserve. It lies between elevations of 482 and 502 feet above sea level and includes a large level bottomland with adjacent uplands. A 670-foot boardwalk above the wet swamp provides easy access for all visitors. Analysis of a fossilized pollen sequence obtained from a 5-foot soil core of the mucky bottomland has shown the swamp to be between 10,000 and 12,000 years old. The drier upland areas are almost entirely covered by large hardwood species, such as northern red oak (*Quercus rubra* var. *borealis*), white oak (*Q. alba*), sugar maple (*Acer saccharum*), and black cherry (*Prunus serotina*). White-tailed deer (*Odocoileus virginianus*) inhabit the swamp, as do red and gray foxes (*Vulpes fulva* and *Urocyon cinereoargenteus*) and eastern coyotes (*Canis latrans*). In addition to red-tailed hawks (*Buteo jamaicensis*) and green-backed herons (*Butorides striatus*), the swamp also supports a rookery for great blue herons (*Ardea herodias*).

Begin your hike at the parking area on the Entrance Trail. Af-

188 👤 *Walks in Nature's Empire*

ter a few yards you will see a short unmarked trail on your right. This leads to the shore of the duck pond, where a chorus of bullfrogs (*Rana catesbeiana*) will serenade you. Returning to the Entrance Trail and turning right (west) you will soon reach the sign for the Song Bird Trail. This trail hooks back onto Deer Run, which serves as the easement road for Rochester Gas & Electric. At Deer Run, take a left and proceed to the boardwalk. A rather friendly grouse may come out to greet you at this point—there were sightings of this curious bird on the day we visited, but we were not favored with its presence.

Take a right onto the boardwalk and through the heart of the swamp. Note the variety of cattails and swamp milkweed (*Asclepias incarnata*), as well as an invasive exotic species known as purple loosestrife (*Lythrum salicaria*). Snapping turtles (*Chelydra serpentina*) and raccoons (*Procyon lotor*) are both present here, so be careful to stay on the boardwalk. This is also a perfect place from which to see and hear woodpeckers, sora rails (*Porzana carolina*), and the ubiquitous red-winged blackbirds (*Agelaius phoeniceus*).

The boardwalk takes you to the northern tip of Weasel Way, where the predominant flowers are marsh marigold (*Caltha palustris*), blue cohosh (*Caulophyllum thalictroides*), and spicebush (*Lindera benzoin*). Fox and weasels (*Mustela* spp.) both frequent this part of the preserve. At the juncture of Weasel Way and Warbler Fen, take another left onto the latter. As the name implies, you should be on the lookout for cerulean (*Dendroica cerulea*) and other warblers along this fern-covered stretch of trail. You may also see red-bellied woodpeckers (*Centurus carolinus*) and scarlet tanagers (*Piranga olivacea*), if you are lucky.

Continue straight onto and into the Hermit Walk. We did not sight a hermit during our visit, although local legend has it that this was indeed once the home of a gentleman who wanted to "get away from the world." In the evening, you might hear a great horned owl (*Bubo virginianus*)—listen for their distinctive call,

Ruffed grouse (*Bonasa umbellus*)

"Hoo, hoo hoo, HOO HOO"—and the drumming of ruffed grouse (*Bonasa umbellus*). This drier stretch of the swamp is prime habitat for trees such as red oak (*Q. rubra*), sugar maple, American beech (*Fagus grandifolia*), and tulip tree (*Liriodendron tulipifera*).

Following the Hermit Walk, you will come to the aptly named Meadows Trail, which has the appearance of an old Native American footpath, although our source could not confirm this notion (it was more likely made by more recent visitors). Hawks and owls enjoy these meadows, feeding on the small mammals that forage among the meadow plants. When we visited there was a plethora of moths and butterflies that seemed to powder the grasses and wildflowers. At the edge of the meadows you will find the Way Pond Trail, which will take you, rather logically, to Way Pond. Blue flag iris (*Iris versicolor*) and cattails (*Typha* spp.) abound at the edge of the pond, and you are likely to see blue-winged teals (*Anas discors*), mallards (*A. platyrhynchos*), and wood ducks (*Aix sponsa*), along with kingfishers (*Megaceryle* spp.) and green-backed and great blue herons (*Butorides striatus* and *Ardea herodias*). In the fall, cedar waxwings (*Bombycilla cedrorum*) come here for the fruit of the prickly ash (*Zanthoxylum americanum*) and elderberry (*Sambucus canadensis*).

Retrace your steps as far back as the fork of Warbler Fen and Trillium Trail, where you will want to take a left onto the Trillium. This 0.16-mile stretch will bring you back to Deer Run (where you should take a left back to the Entrance Trail). Along here you will see the waxy-white flowers of large-flowered trillium (*Trillium grandiflorum*), as well as Jack-in-the-pulpit (*Arisaema triphyllum*) and trout-lily (*Erythronium americanum*), so-called because the markings on its leaves resemble the markings of brook trout. This tour takes roughly 1 hour.

A number of public, guided hikes are scheduled throughout the year; call the Central and Western New York Chapter for details (see appendix 2).

ACQUISITION

The initial parcel was donated by the estate of Fletcher Steele in 1971; additional acreage was acquired from 1977 to 1993.

DIRECTIONS

At the intersection of I-490 and I-590 east of Rochester, take I-590 north 1 mile to NY 286. Drive east on NY 286 approximately 4.9 miles and then turn left (north) onto Jackson Road and proceed for 0.55 mile. The entrance to the sanctuary is indicated by a wooden sign on the west side of Jackson Road, just north of the Monroe County Sheriff's substation. Turn left and follow the narrow driveway, passing to the left of the house at the end of the drive. Park in the graveled lot (closed in winter). Please do not park in the driveway at any time. (Central and Western New York Chapter)

33 *Moss Lake Preserve*

CANEADEA, ALLEGHENY COUNTY

82.23 ACRES (Plus 7-acre conservation easement)

 The Nature Conservancy's Western New York Chapter was founded in 1958 to protect this natural area from commercial development (the chapter merged with its Central New York counterpart
30 years later). The preserve includes a 15-acre dwarf shrub bog
surrounded by glacial moraine, formed as the last glaciers re-
treated and melted. The decaying bog plants and mosses have left
behind a peat deposit, and a sphagnum mat has grown steadily in
from the shore until it now covers much of the open water.

Plants such as bog laurel (*Kalmia polifolia*), round-leaved sundew (*Drosera rotundifolia*), and spatulate-leaved sundew (*D. inter-
media*) grow particularly well in the acidic environment afforded
by the sphagnum mat, and the prolific leatherleaf (*Chamaedaphne
calyculata*) helps knit the entire mat together. When we visited in
July, the greater bladderwort (*Utricularia vulgaris*) was in bloom,
and resembled a floating yellow field atop the surface of the bog
mat. Like pitcher plants, bladderworts are insectivores, and clever
ones at that: Tiny bladderlike vents are located on the plant's roots
and, when touched by water insect passersby, the bladders in-
flate—sucking in both water and the unwitting prey. Once inside,

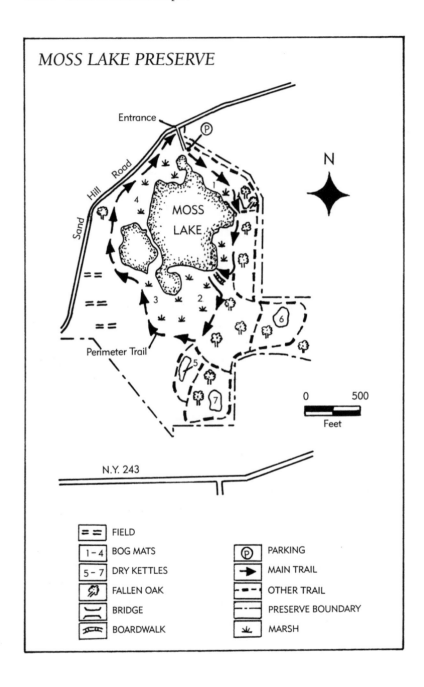

MOSS LAKE PRESERVE

Entrance

MOSS LAKE

Sand Hill Road

Perimeter Trail

N.Y. 243

N

☰ FIELD	
1 – 4 BOG MATS	℗ PARKING
5 – 7 DRY KETTLES	➡ MAIN TRAIL
FALLEN OAK	- - - OTHER TRAIL
BRIDGE	PRESERVE BOUNDARY
BOARDWALK	MARSH

0   500
Feet

the trapped insect cannot get out, and is soon digested.

Given the anecdotal history of Moss Lake, you would expect to have such a strange and dangerous plant here; odd things have been reported at the lake, including an unexplained splashing and agitation of the water surface in 1882 that was witnessed by Harrison Bacon, grandson of the original owner, Jesse Bacon.

Jesse Bacon, a Methodist minister born in 1796, and his wife, Catherine Harris, settled on a 127-acre farm near Moss Lake in 1857. One of their 10 children built a large white farmhouse overlooking the lake in 1894. Moss Lake was then known as Bullhead Pond, apparently due to the great fishing during a time when this pond was stocked with fish. Peat moss was harvested out of the bog during the 1880s—hence its current name—and then started again in 1939 when it was trucked to Olean for drying. Water was also removed from the pond through an elaborate pipeline that led to a nearby watering station for steam engines of the Buffalo & Susquehanna Railroad. Around 1956, Elsie Hotchkiss, the great-granddaughter of Jesse Bacon, and her husband Orville, turned down a large sum to open up the lake for extensive mechanized peat harvesting. Instead, they sold the property to The Nature Conservancy to ensure its long-term preservation as a natural area.

The best way to see Moss Lake is to walk its circumference. Starting at the trailhead, proceed into a heavily wooded area. You will reach the U-shaped boardwalk that extends out onto the mat after about 1500 feet of trail. The boardwalk allows you to experience the bog mat firsthand, and to get a closer view of the more than 75 species of birds that have been recorded at this National Natural Landmark. Moss Lake was so designated in 1973.

Keep to the right on the trail once you leave the boardwalk to take the Perimeter Trail. (There are other trails that lead to the dry kettle areas south of the lake and visitors are free to wander them, but be aware that these trails are not clearly marked, so you should be sure to note some landmarks.) If you stick to the Perimeter

PHOTOGRAPH © THE NATURE CONSERVANCY/ANDREW ZEPP

Bog mat, Moss Lake

Trail, you will get a clear idea of the lake's beauty and functions. Be on the lookout for herons, yellow-bellied flycatchers (*Empidonax flaviventris*), and pied-billed grebes (*Podilymbus podiceps podiceps*). The Perimeter Trail takes about 40 minutes to complete.

ACQUISITION

The initial purchase was made in 1958; a gift of fee on 1.13 acres and easement on 7 acres was made by Franklin Babbit in 1990.

DIRECTIONS

From the New York State Thruway (I-90) take exit 54 outside of Buffalo and drive southeast about 15 miles on NY 400 to US 20A. Go east on US 20A about 29 miles to Warsaw, and then south about 25 miles on NY 19 to Houghton. From the intersection of NY 19 and Genesee Street in Houghton, drive 1.4 miles south on NY 19. Turn right onto Sand Hill Road and drive 0.9 mile up the hill to the sanctuary on the left side of the road. (Central and Western New York Chapter)

DEER LICK SANCTUARY

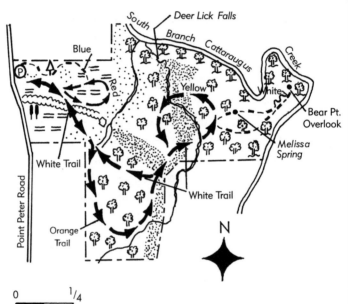

Deer Lick Falls

South Branch Cattaraugus Creek

Blue

Red

Yellow

White

Bear Pt. Overlook

Melissa Spring

White Trail

White Trail

Point Peter Road

Orange Trail

N

0   1/4
Mile

MAIN TRAIL

SECONDARY TRAIL

OTHER TRAIL

PRESERVE BOUNDARY

GAS WELL

MEADOW

SCOTCH PINE

PARKING

CATTAILS

HEMLOCK RAVINE

BEECH, MAPLE
UPLAND FOREST

STREAMSIDE BEECH
MAPLE, RED OAK

HEDGEROW BLACK LOCUST

SHRUB MAPLES
WHITE ASH, APPLE

VERY STEEP TERRAIN

34 Deer Lick Sanctuary

 The northern boundary of this 400-acre mix of forest, abandoned pasture, and open meadow coincides with the southern boundary of New York State's Zoar Valley Multiple Use Area. The sandy glacial soils and the warming influence of Lake Erie allow certain Carolinian zone plants such as eastern red cedar (*Juniperus virginiana*) and cucumber-tree (*Magnolia acuminata*) to grow here; the rising level of the Allegheny plateau makes it conducive to cooler climate species such as eastern hemlock (*Tsuga canadensis*).

Although this confluence of habitats is convenient for wildlife, the same cannot be said for human habitation. While the relatively steep grades and fairly poor soils precluded most farming practices, the production of potash—made from leeching the ashes of burnt oak, maple, beech, and birch trees—and tannin garnered from the bark of hemlocks were two of the few profitable ventures pursued at Deer Lick. The most important resource, however, as the early settlers saw it, was the dense stand of virgin white pine (*Pinus strobus*). The long, straight pine trunks, sometimes over 170 feet tall and 5 feet in diameter, made perfect ships' masts. The trees were cut and shipped to Pittsburgh along the

Deer Lick Falls

nearby Allegheny River, and later on the Erie Canal. This practice lasted until the early 1900s, by which time the old growth pine was virtually exhausted. Area residents continued to harvest the remaining hardwoods until the Conservancy acquired the property in 1960.

There are five color-coded trails on the preserve, and the best way we found to get a complete picture of the sanctuary is to walk a combination of the trails, beginning with the White Trail. Follow this past a series of hedgerows, through a meadow, and into the woods, where you can turn right onto the Orange Trail. This will take you to a hilly, forested area running parallel to Deer Lick Creek, and will eventually loop back around to the White Trail. This part of the trail can be extremely muddy, especially if mountain bikers have been using it, as was the case when we visited. Bicycles and other vehicles are *not* permitted on the Conservancy's trails for just this reason: The damage caused by excessive and thoughtless use can be devastating to trails and rare species habitat.

The White Trail fords the slow-running creek before climbing along a "dry" runoff that extends into the hardwood forest and, before joining the Yellow Trail to the left of Melissa Spring, the White Trail reaches the highest elevation on the preserve (1348 feet). The White Trail continues through the ravine forest and terminates at Bear Point Overlook, with a view of Cattaraugus Creek and, when the trees are bare, the 120-foot Bridal Veil Falls. Retrace your steps back to Melissa Spring, where you should pick up the Yellow Trail. Note the abundance of ferns encouraged by the moist, cool area around the spring. The Yellow Trail then swings west-southwest and down into a ravine by the creekside once again. There is another ford to be negotiated in this ravine, so be alert. The ford is approximately 0.16 mile south of Deer Lick Falls, which you can hear from the trail. Keep your eyes open for the yellow blazes, because the trail switchbacks can get confusing here.

You will rejoin the White Trail for a stretch and here you can either continue back to the parking area, or turn right onto the Red Trail through an open meadow (keep to the right of the gas well). This "trail" through the open meadows and along the top of a forested ravine is poorly marked, so you may want to have a compass along. Through the meadow grasses you will reach the White Trail again after about 1.1 miles. The entire loop takes approximately 2.5 hours. Deer Lick is a National Natural Landmark (1969).

ACQUISITION

This aquisition is made up of gifts from Evelyn and S.G. Alverson (1960); J.S. Wells (1960); Herbert F. Darling (1964). The Conservancy also purchased the 226-acre Goodemote Farm in 1960.

DIRECTIONS

From the New York State Thruway (I-90), take exit 57 in Hamburg and drive south on US 62 through North Collins to Gowanda. Or, from Elmira and points east, drive west on NY 17 until 2 miles beyond Salamanca and turn northwest on NY 353. Follow NY 353 about 25 miles to Dayton and turn right on US 62 for 4 miles to Gowanda. From Main Street (US 62) in Gowanda, turn east onto Water Street at the bridge over the South Branch of the Cattaraugus Creek. Continue 0.6 mile to Broadway (County Route 4) just beyond the railroad crossing. Go south (right) on Broadway to Point Peter Road, turn left, and continue past Forty Road about 0.5 mile to the sanctuary. (Central and Western New York Chapter)

35 *French Creek Preserve*

MINA, CHAUTAUQUA COUNTY
90 ACRES

 French Creek begins in the foothills of the Allegheny Plateau in southern Chautauqua County, before meandering through farm and forest land into Pennsylvania, where it becomes the size of a small river, and then empties into the Allegheny River. It is home to at least 66 species of fish, including 15 that are considered rare in New York State and three that are globally rare: spotted darter (*Etheostoma maculatum*), black redhorse (*Moxostoma duquesnei*), and longhead darter (*Percina macrocephala*). In addition, the creek supports a number of freshwater mussels, one of which is found nowhere else in the state. Downstream in Pennsylvania, a recent survey identified 25 distinct mussel species within French Creek, including clubshell and northern riffleshell mussels (*Pleurobema clava* and *Epioblasma torulosa*). There are more species of mussels in French Creek than are found throughout the entire continent of Europe.

The 70-square-mile watershed of upper French Creek sprawls across five townships. The landscape around the creek reflects generations of human influence upon the land, and these influences are still being felt by the creek. Sediments, as well as pesticides and

FRENCH CREEK PRESERVE

N

French Creek

Tributary

0   500

Feet

County Route 4

MIXED HARDWOOD FOREST

FLOOD PLAIN (MIXED HARDWOOD AND FLOOD PLAIN FOREST)

SUCCESSIONAL WET PASTURE / BRUSH

GAS WELL

FALLOW CULTIVATED FIELD

FALLOW FIELD

PARKING

FUTURE MARSH

PRESERVE BOUNDARY

MAIN TRAIL

PHOTOGRAPH © THE NATURE CONSERVANCY/ANDREW ZEPP

French Creek Preserve

other chemicals, are carried into the creek by rainwater runoff and occasional flooding. Because of these detrimental influences, the Conservancy is trying to protect the entire watershed, and French Creek has been nominated as a multi-state "Last Great Place."

"Last Great Places: An Alliance for People and the Environment" is a conservation program designed to protect outstanding ecosystems in the United States, Latin America, and the Pacific. At each location, the Conservancy is working closely with partners, both public and private, to demonstrate that economic, recreational, and other development can occur where nature is being preserved.

The unfolding strategy to preserve French Creek's integrity involves cooperative efforts with public and private agencies and landowners, specifically those that have the capacity to affect the river through land-use-related activities. Key concerns are the various sources of pollution and sedimentation from such activities as agriculture and other development. The Conservancy is working with willing and concerned landowners throughout the French Creek watershed to ensure the vitality of the creek. Local governments, as well as organizations such as the Natural Resources Conservation Service, will also play an important role in future watershed protection efforts.

The preserve includes 0.75 mile of frontage on both sides of the creek, as well as a portion of a significant tributary stream. The trail begins on an old logging road and courses through a pasture, which is currently being reclaimed by hawthorn trees (*Crataegus* spp.), and a fallow, cultivated field before reaching French Creek itself. This loop trail displays the variety of habitat at the French Creek Preserve. The floodplain forest, found in low-lying areas near the creek, is characterized by sugar and red maples (*Acer saccharum* and *A. rubrum*), hawthorn, and sycamore (*Platanus* sp.),

PARTNERS IN WILDLIFE

To address erosion caused by grazing dairy cattle along a portion of French Creek in Chautauqua County, The Nature Conservancy joined forces with a local dairy farmer and the US Fish and Wildlife Service to fence cattle away from sensitive streamside areas. The farmer gave permission to erect the fence; the Fish and Wildlife Service provided electric fencing and posts through its "Partners in Wildlife" program; and the Conservancy provided the labor. This is only the first of many habitat restoration projects that the Conservancy plans to initiate in the French Creek watershed. Voluntary partnerships like this are the cornerstone of the Conservancy's efforts here.

with a ground layer of sensitive fern (*Onoclea sensibilis*) and spice-bush (*Lindera benzoin*). The trail then winds through a mixed hardwood forest and up along the creekside bluff before returning to the fallow field.

The entire loop takes roughly 1 hour.

ACQUISITION

This 90-acre parcel was purchased in 1990.

DIRECTIONS

From exit 6 on the Southern Tier Expressway (NY 17) near the Village of Sherman, follow NY 76 south for 3.5 miles. Turn right (west) onto County Route 4 and follow this for 5 miles. From the Village of French Creek, near the Peek 'n' Peak Resort and Conference Center, follow County Route 4 north for 2 miles. The preserve entrance is marked by a large wooden sign. (Central and Western New York Chapter)

Appendix 1:
List of Flora and Fauna

🌿 BIRDS

Bittern	American	*Botaurus lentiginosus*
Blackbird	Red-winged	*Agelaius phoeniceus*
Bluebird	Eastern	*Sialia sialis*
Bobwhite		*Colinus virginianus*
Chickadee	Black-capped	*Parus atricapillus*
	Boreal	*Parus hudsonicus*
Cormorant	Double-crested	*Phalacrocorax auritus*
Cowbird	Brown-headed	*Molothrus ater*
Dowitcher	Short-billed	*Limnodromus griseus*
Duck	Black	*Anas rubripes*
	Canvasback	*Aythya valisineria*
	Mallard	*Anas platyrhynchos*
	Wood	*Aix sponsa*
Eagle	Bald	*Haliaeetus leucocephalus*
Egret	Great	*Casmerodius albus*
	Snowy	*Egretta thula*
Falcon	Peregrine	*Falco peregrinus*
Flycatcher	Olive-sided	*Contopus borealis*
	Yellow-bellied	*Empidonax flaviventris*
Goose	Canada	*Branta canadensis*

Goshawk	Northern	*Accipiter gentilis*
Grackle		*Quiscalus* sp.
Grebe	Pied-billed	*Podilymbus podiceps podiceps*
Grosbeak	Rose-breasted	*Pheucticus ludovicianus*
Grouse	Ruffed	*Bonasa umbellus*
	Spruce	*Dendragapus canadensis*
Harrier	Northern	*Circus cyaneus*
Hawk	Broad-winged	*Buteo platypterus platypterus*
	Cooper's	*Accipiter cooperii*
	Red-shouldered	*Buteo lineatus*
	Red-tailed	*Buteo jamaicensis*
	Sharp-shinned	*Accipiter striatus velox*
	Sparrow	*Falco sparverius*
Heron	Black-crowned Night	*Nycticorax nycticorax*
	Great Blue	*Ardea herodias*
	Green-backed	*Butorides striatus*
Hummingbird	Ruby-throated	*Archilochus colubris*
Jay	Blue	*Cyanocitta cristata*
	Gray	*Perisoreus canadensis*
Kestrel	American	*Falco sparverius*
Kingfisher	Eastern Belted	*Megaceryle alcyon*
Kinglet	Golden-crowned	*Regulus satrapa*
Nighthawk	Common	*Chordeiles minor*
Nuthatch	Red-breasted	*Sitta canadensis*
Osprey		*Pandion haliaetus carolinensis*
Owl	Barred	*Strix varia*
	Great Horned	*Bubo virginianus*
	Screech	*Otus asio*
Pewee	Eastern Wood	*Contopus virens*
Pheasant	Ring-necked	*Phasianus colchicus*
Plover	Piping	*Charadrius melodus*
	Semipalmated	*Charadrius semipalmatus*

Raven	Common	*Corvus corax*
Sandpiper	Least	*Calidris minutilla*
	Semipalmated	*Calidris pusilla*
	Upland	*Bartramia longicauda*
Sapsucker	Yellow-billed	*Sphyrapicus varius*
Sora Rail		*Porzana carolina*
Sparrow	House	*Passer domesticus*
Tanager	Scarlet	*Piranga olivacea*
Teal	Blue-winged	*Anas discors*
Tern	Common	*Sterna hirundo hirundo*
	Least	*Sterna albifrons*
	Roseate	*Sterna dougallii*
Thrush	Hermit	*Catharus guttatus*
	Wood	*Hylocichla mustelina*
Veery		*Hylocichla fuscescens*
Vireo	Solitary	*Vireo solitarius*
	Warbling	*Vireo gilvus*
Warbler	Black-and-white	*Mniotilta varia*
	Blackburnian	*Dendroica fusca*
	Blackpoll	*Dendroica striata*
	Cerulean	*Dendroica cerulea*
	Nashville	*Vermivora ruficapilla*
	Prairie	*Dendroica discolor*
	Yellow-rumped	*Dendroica coronata*
Waxwing	Cedar	*Bombycilla cedrorum*
Whip-poor-will		*Caprimulgus vociferous*
Woodpecker	Downy	*Picoides pubescens*
	Hairy	*Picoides villosus*
	Pileated	*Dryocopus pileatus*
	Red-bellied	*Centurus carolinus*
Wren	Winter	*Troglodytes troglodytes*
Yellowlegs	Lesser	*Tringa flavipes*

🍂 MAMMALS

Bat	Indiana	*Myotis sodalis*
	Small-footed	*Myotis leibii*
Bear	Black	*Ursus americanus*
Beaver		*Castor canadensis*
Bobcat		*Lynx rufus*
Chipmunk	Eastern	*Tamias striatus fisheri*
Coyote	Eastern	*Canis latrans*
Deer	White-tailed	*Odocoileus virginianus*
Fisher		*Martes pennanti*
Fox	Gray	*Urocyon cinereoargenteus*
	Red	*Vulpes fulva*
Hare	Snowshoe	*Lepus americanus*
Lemming	Bog	*Synaptomys cooperi*
Mink		*Mustela vison*
Mole	Eastern	*Scalopus aquaticus*
Mouse	Deer	*Peromyscus maniculatus*
Muskrat		*Ondatra zibethica*
Opossum		*Didelphis marsupialis*
Porcupine		*Erethizon dorsatum*
Rabbit	Eastern Cottontail	*Sylvilagus floridanus*
Raccoon		*Procyon lotor*
Shrew	Shorttail	*Blarina brevicauda*
Squirrel	Gray	*Sciurus carolinensis pensylvanicus*
	Red	*Tamiasciurus hudsonicus*
Vole	Boreal Redback	*Clethrionomys gapperi*
	Pine	*Pitymys pinetorum*
Weasel		*Mustela* sp.
Woodrat	Eastern, or Allegheny	*Neotoma floridana*

✿ FISH

Black Redhorse		*Moxostoma duquesnei*
Bluegill (Sunfish)		*Lepomis macrochirus*
Catfish	Bullhead	*Ictalurus nebulosus*
Darter	Long Head	*Percina macrocephala*
	Spotted	*Etheostoma maculatum*
Eel	American	*Anguilla rostrata*
Perch	Yellow	*Perca flavescens*
Pickerel	Chain	*Esox niger*

✿ REPTILES AND AMPHIBIANS

Frog	Bullfrog	*Rana catesbeiana*
	Green	*Rana clamitans*
	Wood	*Rana sylvatica*
Newt	Red-spotted	*Notophthalmus viridescens-viridescens*
Salamander	Mole	*Ambystoma* sp.
	Spotted	*Ambystoma maculatum*
Sea Turtle	Kemps-Ridley	*Lepidochelys kempi*
Toad	Fowler's	*Bufo woodhousei fowleri*
Turtle	Eastern Painted	*Chrysemys picta picta*
	Snapping	*Chelydra serpentina*

✿ INSECTS

Blackfly		*Simulium* sp.
Buckmoth	Coastal Barrens	*Hemileuca maia maia*
Butterfly	Baltimore	*Euphydryas phaeton*
	Karner Blue	*Lycaeides melissa samuelis*
Mosquito		*Aedes* sp.
Moth		*Apharetra purpurea*
		Itame species
		Lithophane lepida lepida

| | | *Xylena thoracica* |
| Underwing | Herodias | *Catocala herodias gerhardi* |

❧ INVERTEBRATES

Mussels	Alewife Floater	*Anodonta implicata*
	Brook Floater	*Alasmidonta varicosa*
	Clubshell	*Pleurobema clava*
	Dwarf Wedgemussel	*Alasmidonta heterodon*
	Northern Riffleshell	*Epioblasma torulosa*
	Ribbed	*Modiolus demissus plicatulus*
Periwinkle		*Littorina palliata*

❧ PLANTS

Algae		*Cladophora*
Anemone	Wood	*Anemone quinquefolia*
Arbutus	Trailing	*Epigaea repens*
Arrowwood		*Viburnum recognitum*
Arum	Arrow	*Sagittaria latifolia*
Ash	Black	*Fraxinus nigra*
	Green	*Fraxinus pennsylvanica*
	Prickly	*Zanthoxylum americanum*
	White	*Fraxinus americana*
Aspen	Quaking	*Populus tremuloides*
Azalea	Swamp	*Rhododendron nudiflorum*
Basswood		*Tilia americana*
Bayberry		*Myrica pensylvanica*
Bearberry		*Arctostaphylos uva-ursi*
Beech	American	*Fagus grandifolia*
Birch	Black	*Betula lenta*
	White, or Paper	*Betula papyrifera*
	Yellow	*Betula alleghanensis*
Bittersweet	Asiatic	*Celastrus orbiculatus*
Blackberry		*Rubus* sp.

Bladderwort	Greater	*Utricularia vulgaris*
Blueberry		*Vaccinium* sp.
	Highbush	*Vaccinium corymbosum*
Bluestem	Big	*Andropogon gerardii*
	Little	*Schizachyrium scoparium*
Buckthorn	Common	*Rhamnus cathartica*
Bugleweed		*Lycopus uniflorus*
Bulrush		*Scirpus atrovirens*
Burnet	Canadian	*Sanguisorba canadensis*
Bush-clover		*Lespedeza capitata*
Buttonbush		*Cephalanthus occidentalis*
Cactus	Prickly-pear	*Opuntia humifusa*
Catbrier		*Smilax rotundifolia*
Cattail		*Typha* sp.
Cedar	Atlantic White	*Chamaecyparis thyoides*
	Eastern Red	*Juniperus virginiana*
	Northern White	*Thuja occidentalis*
Cherry	Black	*Prunus serotina*
Chestnut	American	*Castanea dentata*
Chokeberry		*Aronia* sp.
Cinquefoil	Rough	*Potentilla norvegica*
Clubmoss	Shining	*Huperzia lucidulum*
	Tree or Ground Pine	*Lycopodium obscurum*
Cohosh	Blue	*Caulophyllum thalictroides*
Cord Grass	Salt-meadow	*Spartina patens*
	Saltwater	*Spartina alterniflora*
Cottongrass		*Eriophorum virginicum*
Cranberry	American	*Vaccinium macrocarpon*
Cucumber-tree		*Magnolia acuminata*
Dogwood	Flowering	*Cornus florida*
Dropseed	Prairie	*Sporobolus heterolepis*
Dutchman's Breeches		*Dicentra cucullaria*
Eelgrass		*Zostera marina*

Elder	Saltmarsh-	*Iva frutescens*
Elderberry		*Sambucus canadensis*
Elm	Slippery	*Ulmus rubra*
Fern	Bladder, or Bulblet	*Cystopteris bulbifera*
	Bracken	*Pteridium aquilinum*
	Christmas	*Polystichum acrostichoides*
	Cinnamon	*Osmunda cinnamomea*
	Crested Shield	*Dryopteris cristata*
	Hay-scented	*Dennstaedtia punctilobula*
	Marsh	*Thelypteris palustris*
	Mountain Wood-	*Dryopteris campyloptera*
	New York	*Thelypteris noveboracensis*
	Royal	*Osmunda regalis*
	Sensitive	*Onoclea sensibilis*
	Spinulose Wood-	*Dryopteris carthusiana*
	Walking	*Camptosorus rhizophyllus*
Fir	Balsam	*Abies balsamea*
Fireweed		*Epilobium angustifolium*
Foamflower		*Tiarella cordifolia*
Gall-of-the-Earth		*Prenanthes trifoliolata*
Glasswort		*Salicornia* sp.
Goat's-rue		*Tephrosia virginiana*
Goldenrod		*Solidago* sp.
	Seaside	*Solidago sempervirens*
Goldthread		*Coptis trifolia*
Gum	Black	*Nyssa sylvatica*
Grape	Fox	*Vitis labrusca*
Grass	Beach, or Dune	*Ammophila breviligulata*
	Big Bluestem	*Andropogon gerardii*
	Common Hair-	*Deschampsia flexuosa*
	Little Bluestem	*Schizachyrium scoparium*
	Orchard	*Dactylis glomerata*
	Poverty	*Danthonia spicata*

	Rice Cutgrass	*Leersia oryzoides*
	Salt-meadow Cord	*Spartina patens*
	Saltwater Cord	*Spartina alterniflora*
	Southern Hair-	*Agrostis hiemalis*
	Spike	*Distichlis spicata*
	Timothy	*Phleum pratense*
	Tufted Hair-	*Deschampsia cespitosa*
Greenbriar		*Smilax rotundifolia*
Groundnut		*Apios americana*
Groundsel Tree		*Baccharis halimifolia*
Hairgrass	Common	*Deschampsia flexuosa*
	Southern	*Agrostis hiemalis*
	Tufted	*Deschampsia cespitosa*
Harebell		*Campanula rotundifolia*
Hawthorn		*Crataegus* sp.
Heather	False	*Hudsonia tomentosa*
Hemlock	Eastern	*Tsuga canadensis*
Hepatica	Sharp-lobed	*Hepatica nobilis* var. *acuta*
Hickory		*Carya* sp.
	Bitternut	*Carya cordiformis*
	Pignut	*Carya glabra*
	Shagbark	*Carya ovata*
Hobblebush		*Viburnum lantanoides*
Hog-peanut		*Amphicarpea bracteata*
Holly	Mountain	*Nemopanthus mucronatus*
Honeysuckle		*Lonicera* sp.
Hophornbeam	Eastern	*Ostrya virginiana*
Huckleberry	Black	*Gaylussacia baccata*
Indian-paintbrush		*Castilleja coccinea*
Indian-pipe		*Monotropa uniflora*
Iris	Blue Flag	*Iris versicolor*
Jack-in-the-pulpit		*Arisaema triphyllum*
Joe-Pye Weed		*Eupatorium maculatum*

Juniper		*Juniperus communis*
Laurel	Bog	*Kalmia polifolia*
	Mountain	*Kalmia latifolia*
	Sheep	*Kalmia angustifolia*
Leatherleaf		*Chamaedaphne calyculata*
Lettuce	Blue	*Lactuca biennis*
Lichen		*Cladonia* sp.
		Usnea sp.
	Common Redstem	*Pleurozium schreberi*
	Haircap	*Polytrichum* sp.
	Iceland Moss	*Cetraria arenaria*
	Pink Earth	*Baeomyces roseus*
	Reindeer	*Cladina* sp.
Locust	Black	*Robinia pseudo–acacia*
Loosestrife	Purple	*Lythrum salicaria*
	Whorled	*Lysimachia quadrifolia*
Lupine	Wild	*Lupinus perennis*
Maple	Red	*Acer rubrum*
	Striped	*Acer pensylvanicum*
	Sugar	*Acer saccharum*
Marigold	Marsh	*Caltha palustris*
Mayflower	Canada	*Maianthemum canadense*
Milkweed	Swamp	*Asclepias incarnata*
Moosewood		*Acer pensylvanicum*
Moss	Outboard Motor	*Tortella tortuosa*
	White Cushion	*Leucobryum glaucum*
	Worm	*Bryum cespiticium*
Oak	Black	*Quercus velutina*
	Bur	*Quercus macrocarpa*
	Chestnut	*Quercus montana*
	Dwarf Chinquapin	*Quercus prinoides*
	Northern Red	*Quercus rubra* var. *borealis*
	Post	*Quercus stellata*

	Red	*Quercus rubra*
	Scarlet	*Quercus coccinea*
	Scrub	*Quercus ilicifolia*
	Swamp White	*Quercus bicolor*
	White	*Quercus alba*
Orchid	White-fringed	*Platanthera blephariglottis*
Pennyroyal	False	*Trichostema brachiatum*
Pepperbush	Sweet	*Clethra alnifolia*
Pickerelweed		*Pontederia cordata*
Pine	Eastern White	*Pinus strobus*
	Jack	*Pinus banksiana*
	Pitch	*Pinus rigida*
	Red	*Pinus resinosa*
	Scotch	*Pinus sylvestris*
Pitcher Plant	Northern	*Sarracenia purpurea*
Plum	Beach	*Prunus maritima*
Pogonia	Whorled Large	*Isotria verticillata*
Poison Ivy		*Toxicodendron radicans*
Prairie Smoke		*Geum triflorum*
Redroot	Prairie	*Ceanothus herbaceus*
Rhododendron	Giant	*Rhododendron maximum*
Rice Cutgrass		*Leersia oryzoides*
Riverweed		*Podostemum ceratophyllum*
Rosebay	Lapland	*Rhododendron lapponicum*
Rosemary	Bog	*Andromeda polifolia* var. *glaucophylla*
Sarsaparilla	Wild	*Aralia nudicaulis*
Sea-lavender		*Limonium carolinianum*
Seaweed	Brown	*Fucus* sp.
Sedge	Chestnut	*Carex castanea*
	Cottongrass	*Eriophorum virginicum*
	Crawe's	*Carex crawei*
	Few-seeded	*Carex oligosperma*

	Houghton's Umbrella	*Cyperus houghtonii*
	Pennsylvania	*Carex pensylvanica*
	Troublesome	*Carex molesta*
Shadbush	Nantucket	*Amelanchier* X *nantuck-etensis*
	Serviceberry	*Amelanchier canadensis*
Silverweed		*Potentilla anserina* ssp. *pacifica*
Skunk Cabbage		*Symplocarpus foetidus*
Smartweed	Water	*Polygonum amphibium* var. *emersum*
Sphagnum Moss		*Sphagnum* sp.
Spicebush		*Lindera benzoin*
Spiraea		*Spiraea* sp.
Spruce	Black	*Picea mariana*
	Norway	*Picea abies*
	Red	*Picea rubens*
Strawberry	Barren	*Waldsteinia fragarioides*
Sumac	Staghorn	*Rhus typhina*
Sundew	Round-leaved	*Drosera rotundifolia*
	Spatulate-leaved	*Drosera intermedia*
Sweet-fern		*Comptonia peregrina*
Sycamore		*Platanus occidentalis*
Tamarack	or American Larch	*Larix laricina*
	or European Larch	*Larix decidua*
Tea	Labrador	*Ledum groenlandicum*
Timothy		*Phleum pratense*
Touch-me-not	Spotted	*Impatiens capensis*
Trillium	Large-flowered	*Trillium grandiflorum*
Trout-lily		*Erythronium americanum*
Tulip Tree		*Liriodendron tulipifera*
Tupelo	Black	*Nyssa sylvatica*
Twinflower		*Linnaea borealis*

Venus Flytrap		*Dionaea muscipula*
Virginia Creeper		*Parthenocissus quinquefolia*
Willow	Swamp	*Salix nigra*
Winterberry		*Ilex verticillata*
Wintergreen		*Gaultheria procumbens*
Witch-hazel		*Hamamelis virginiana*
Witch-hobble		*Viburnum lantanoides*
Yew	Ground	*Taxus canadensis*

Appendix 2:
The Nature Conservancy
Offices in New York State

🍂 **NEW YORK REGIONAL OFFICE**

91 Broadway
Albany, NY 12204
518-463-6133
Fax: 518-463-6160

🍂 **NEW YORK CITY OFFICE**

1500 Broadway, Suite 808
New York, NY 10036
212-997-1880
Fax: 212-997-8451

🍂 **SOUTH FORK/SHELTER ISLAND CHAPTER**

3 Railroad Ave.
PO Box 5125
East Hampton, NY 11937
516-329-7689
Fax: 516-329-0215

❧ **LONG ISLAND CHAPTER**

250 Lawrence Hill Rd.
Cold Spring Harbor, NY 11724
516-367-3225
Fax: 516-367-4715

❧ **LOWER HUDSON CHAPTER**

41 South Moger Ave.
Mt. Kisco, NY 10549
914-244-3271
Fax: 914-244-3275

❧ **EASTERN NEW YORK CHAPTER**

251 River St.
Troy, NY 12180
518-272-0195
Fax: 518-272-0298

❧ **ADIRONDACK NATURE CONSERVANCY
AND ADIRONDACK LAND TRUST**

PO Box 65
Keene Valley, NY 12943
518-576-2082
Fax: 518-576-4203

❧ **CENTRAL AND WESTERN NEW YORK CHAPTER**

315 Alexander St.
Rochester, NY 14604
716-546-8030
Fax: 716-546-7825

❧ **NEW YORK NATURAL HERITAGE PROGRAM**

700 Troy-Schenectady Rd.

Latham, NY 12110-2400
518-783-3932
Fax: 518-783-3916

🍂 **THE NATURE CONSERVANCY INTERNATIONAL HEADQUARTERS**
1815 North Lynn St.
Arlington, VA 22209
703-841-5300
Fax: 703-841-1283

Appendix 3:
A Note on the Author

Scott Edward Anderson is a poet and frequent contributor to *The Bloomsbury Review* and *E: The Environmental Magazine*, among other publications. He currently serves as the Director of Development for The Nature Conservancy's New York Lower Hudson Chapter. He lives with his wife, Anne Dubuisson, in New York's Hudson River valley.

More Books from The Countryman Press

In addition to enjoying The Nature Conservancy's preserves, there's lots to do in New York. Here's a sample of books about activities in the Empire State from The Countryman Press.

Hiking

50 Hikes in Central New York: Hikes and Backpacking Trips from the Western Adirondacks to the Finger Lakes (second edition), by William P. Ehling, $14.00

50 Hikes in the Hudson Valley: From the Catskills to the Taconics, and from the Ramapos to the Helderbergs (second edition), by Barbara McMartin and Peter Kick with James McMartin Long, $14.00

Fifty Hikes in the Adirondacks: Short Walks, Day Trips, and Backpacks Throughout the Park (second edition), by Barbara McMartin, $13.00

Fifty Hikes in Western New York: Walks and Day Hikes from the Cattaraugus Hills to the Genessee Valley, by William Ehling, $13.00

Walks & Rambles

Walks & Rambles in Dutchess and Putnam Counties: A Guide to Ecology and History in Eastern Hudson Valley Parks, by Peggy Turco, $11.00

Walks & Rambles in Westchester and Fairfield Counties: A Nature Lover's Guide to 36 Parks and Sanctuaries (second edition), by Katherine S. Anderson, revised by Peggy Turco, $11.00

Biking

25 Bicycle Tours in the Adirondacks: Road Adventures in the East's Largest Wilderness, by Bill McKibben, Sue Halpern, Mitchell Hay, and Barbara Lemmel, $13.00

20 Bicycle Tours in and around New York City (revised edition), by Dan Carlinsky and David Heim, $11.00

25 Bicycle Tours in the Hudson Valley: Scenic Rides from Saratoga to West Point, by Howard Stone, $10.00

Cross-Country Skiing

Adirondack Cross-Country Skiing: A Guide to Seventy Trails, by Dennis Conroy with Shirley Matzke, $16.00

Travel

The Hudson Valley and Catskill Mountains: An Explorer's Guide, by Joanne Michaels and Mary-Margaret Barile, $15.00

We offer a variety of fiction and nonfiction. Our books are available through bookstores, or they may be ordered directly from the publisher. For shipping and handling costs, to order, or for a complete catalog, please call 800/245-4151 or write The Countryman Press, Inc., PO Box 175, Woodstock, VT 05091.

The Nature Conservancy Membership Contribution Form

☐ Yes, I want to join The Nature Conservancy and support its efforts to protect rare species and the places they live. I've enclosed a tax-deductible contribution of $_____ ($25 minimum for membership).

☐ I am already a member, but want to further support the efforts of The Nature Conservancy. Enclosed is my check for $_____.

☐ My employer (or spouse's employer) will match my contribution to the Conservancy. Enclosed is my matching gift form.

☐ Please send me more information about The Nature Conservancy's work in my area. I live in _____ County of New York.

Name _____

Address _____

City _____ State _____ Zip _____

Phone # _____

Please send your tax-deductible check, made payable to The Nature Conservancy, along with this form, to: The Nature Conservancy, New York Regional Office, 91 Broadway, Albany, NY 12204; (518) 463-6160.

[NYSPG]